IMMIGRANT

To Laleh & Keri

Thank you for being
here @ the New Dominion
Bookshop ☺

#bebold

IMMIGRANT

COURAGE REQUIRED

GOLARA HAGHTALAB

IN-BOOK ILLUSTRATIONS: PARISA ERKIN

NEW DEGREE PRESS

COPYRIGHT © 2021 GOLARA HAGHTALAB

IMMIGRANT

COURAGE REQUIRED

ISBN   978-1-63676-497-9   *Paperback*

978-1-63730-417-4   *Kindle Ebook*

978-1-63730-418-1   *Ebook*

*To all those who are on the path of
self-discovery to recreate their lives.*

You got this!

Soul
March 17, 2020

I type as if I play piano
But I never played piano before
Oh wait
I did
One time
I played "Fur Elise" for my soul
That's all I learned
And that's all I knew
But still, when I type
I feel like I am playing the piano
An unknown song no one ever heard of
Just for me
For my own
Lovely
Soul...

CONTENTS

———

AUTHOR'S NOTE

———

My name is Golara Haghtalab, and I am the author of *Immigrant*. In 2011, after winning two diversity visa lotteries, my family and I immigrated from Iran to the US. It was pure luck and my parents' personal and financial sacrifices that brought our entire family to this country and allowed me to have the best education and plenty of opportunities for personal and professional growth. In 2020, following the recent social justice movements in the US, millions of people came out on the streets to ask for change. They risked their health and well-being regardless of the deadly global pandemic taking many lives during the same year. Because of that, I, too, felt the urgency to speak up and stand with the millions in solidarity. My way of showing support was writing.

After careful consideration, I decided the best story to tell would be of overcoming change and transition. So, I decided to share my story as an immigrant. While my journey is only one of the many immigrant experiences in the world and the US, I still thought it could embody change and transformation. My life's path was giving me the chance to do something bigger than myself to benefit others. My decision to strengthen the movement for social change made it necessary for my book, *Immigrant*, to be published this year. The current dialogues around diversity, inclusion and equity required all the support there is in the world. Our world was changing, and I wanted to help this global transition to happen.

Within the chapters of this book, you'll explore sixteen vivid thoughts and flashbacks during a day in my life, a thirty-year-old immigrant in the US. I decided to become a character in my book to acknowledge my thoughts actively and bravely track them down to their origins in the past. Once the source of each thought was identified, I tried to weave the lessons learned and my realizations back into the present-day event to achieve resolution. Evaluating whether I should keep or drop the behavior that took me down memory lane allowed me to make decisions for myself in a more meaningful way than I did before.

In this way, I enabled myself to untie some of my psychological knots, thought by thought and chapter by chapter, while sharing my findings with others who might be in the same boat as me. My character in this book juggles multiple languages and cultures in her mind and cannot express herself. She constantly feels as if she is losing and learning and figuring it all out simultaneously. Her journey reshapes her identity as she tries to make sense of basic conversations and interactions with people from different cultures, backgrounds, and identities. Immigration is a beast, and she is on a quest to face it and master her life in a new country: the US.

You might already know that the United States has a larger immigrant population than any other country, with 45 million immigrants as of 2018. This represents 16.5 percent of about 272 million international migrants globally in

2019, equating to about 4 percent of the global population. These numbers do not consider the estimated 740 million internal migrants in 2009 (U.N., World Migration Report 2020). These numbers make up for many people who might be experiencing the same obstacles as I am. Knowing this, I was encouraged to keep writing my book until it was complete and published.

In addition to the main topic of immigration, I sprinkle in stories about identity, race, gender, and death in different chapters. Each of these topics is dear to me because they also embody change in their unique ways. After all, this is a book about change and adaptation. In reading this book, I hope that you will discover the resiliency of an immigrant and her journey to self-discovery in a new country. Furthermore, I hope to instill in you the same passion and excitement for diverse perspectives and the lessons of enduring change and achieving adaptation. Ultimately, I want you to see this book as a friend who helps you unlock your superpowers when faced with a new situation that is unknown to you.

PART 1:

WINGS TO
THE SKY

———

PICTURES

It is possible that a picture will move far away from nature and yet find its way back to reality. The faculty of memory, experience at a distance produces pictorial associations.

PAUL KLEE

It was still dark when my eyes opened. I tried to blink the sleep away while catching a glance at the alarm clock on my nightstand. The clock had just hit 5:00 am. My mind started to wonder about what had woken me as I pushed myself partway up and leaned back against my headboard. My eyes moved to the window, and a feeling of euphoria filled my chest. The view was nothing short of magical. Deep blues and sharp yellows intertwined tidily as the sun emerged out of the night sky. The beauty took my breath away. I made to reach for my phone to capture this magic, but I couldn't get my eyes to leave the window. The next thing I knew, I had fallen back into a deep sleep.

The alarm went off at 7:00 am. Once again, I was awakened from a dream half-remembered. Reaching for my phone, I hoped to find a picture of the sky. There it was, a set of blurry images in the phone gallery. For a moment, I tried to remember the dream I had last night. I couldn't grasp a vivid memory of it whatsoever. A little disappointed and while still in bed, I jumped from a social media account to another on my phone. Deep down, I was restlessly hoping someone was looking to reach out to me. No luck! Setting aside the phone, I stayed in bed for a little longer with my eyes closed. Finally, the sunlight disturbed my eyes just enough for me to give up napping. I got out of the bed and put on my slippers. The clock read 7:19 am.

Like a robot in need of its morning fuel, I marched straight to my desk, and arched my back to reach the button that turned on the work laptop. *It takes a full twenty minutes for this thing to start.* Once I accomplished the important work-related task like a true workaholic, it was time for my next stop, the kitchen. When I say kitchen, I mean a small rectangle designed to function as a space for cooking, preparing food, and most importantly brewing speedy coffee in my tiny DC condo. It is exactly parallel to my work desk, so as I turned my back, practically, I was in the middle of my so-called kitchen space. Almost like a robot, I filled the kettle with water and placed it on the fire. While paused in front of the oven for a moment, I turned my head to glance out of the kitchen window.

It is Tuesday, November 17, 2020, and I live in a world where we all suffer from the circumstances of the global pandemic caused by a coronavirus. In March 2020, the World Health Organization (WHO) declared the COVID-19 outbreak a pandemic, and everyone in the world was encouraged to stay at home. The virus responsible for the global pandemic is known to be the most deadly and contagious virus known to this day. There are thousands, if not millions, who are affected by the illness, globally. Governments across the globe are setting lockdowns to ensure social distancing in their nations. Our president and former media personality, Donald Trump, calls it the Chinese Virus, blaming China for creating and spreading the illness on purpose.

The coronavirus was first reported in Wuhan, China. Many of Trump's loyal followers agree with him and his interesting comments about global issues, including the Chinese Virus. Trump and some of his followers do not believe we should wear masks to prevent this global illness from spreading. My thoughts on all of this are that once the battle with the COVID-19 virus is over, I will feel no less than a full-on trauma survivor. The side effects of loneliness are the least a few billion of us have to deal with because of this pandemic. I will not be surprised if someone says that loneliness's impact on mortality is the same as smoking many cigarettes a day and can cause early death. Sometimes I feel like all of us COVID-19 survivors will probably suffer from mental and emotional issues caused by this global trauma for years to come. I genuinely hope to be wrong with my statement.

Working from home is the new normal enforced on many of us, including myself. Both work and home lives are pretty twisted into each other, and on top of that, I had to turn thirty all alone. Even remembering my birthday is painful. All my life, I dreamt of turning thirty, driving a convertible Jaguar, and having $5 million in my bank account. So, it was a little bit of a bummer to be alone, not as wealthy, and in lockdown two days ago, on my thirtieth birthday. *Cheer up, gal-pal*, I declared with an enthusiastic voice; *it is time to pee* as I hit the road to my bathroom.

As I simultaneously pulled my pants up and brushed my teeth, for a moment, I thought it was my father's older sister that was looking back at me intensely in the mirror. I panicked, jumped back, and hit the bathroom door behind me like a clumsy cat. *What the hell!* My back was hurting from hitting the edge of the door. With a toothbrush still in my mouth, I paused, closed my eyes, and tried to regulate my breathing.

My father's older sister immigrated to Turkey years before I was born. Growing up, everyone thought I was her look-alike. We shared the same round face shape, brown eyes, olive skin, and an intense, determined gaze that runs in my dad's side of the family. I remember her as an attractive woman who wore well-made, colorful dresses and had a unique taste in picking accessories to go with her style. When she walked under the sun, her hair glowed a glossy blackish-blue. Her confidence radiated out of her skin like moonlight, and her nails were always done. I envied her jewelry box filled with the latest 90s trends. She embraced womanhood.

Every summer, she visited Iran with her two sons. Each year she seemed to be more lost between the two worlds she lived in. Her divided world included a tiny one, where her mother and relatives belonged. The other one was a vast and connected world, where her friends and husband belonged. Sometimes, she would forget to wear a scarf over her head. Other times, she would go out of the house without wearing the unique embroidered traditional inch tall hat called *Annaqi* that our married women wear to show others they are not single.

My aunt's cigarettes and smoking habits were yet another unique thing about her because I didn't know any other woman around me who dared to smoke in public. She would freely smoke her cigarettes in the backyard of my grand-mother's house while sipping on her cup of coffee. Every time she visited us in Iran, "I miss my mother" was her reason for returning each time. Every afternoon, after lunch, I would see her leaning on my grandmother's doorsteps by the kitchen, looking straight at the fig tree across the lawn, and smoking her cigarettes. I couldn't imagine where her train of thought traveled as a child. All I could do was to stare at her from under the orange tree I used to play under with my dolls. I would almost study her for the entire time she smoked her cigarettes one by one and took a sip of her sexy, delicious-looking cup of coffee.

One day, I got too close to her coffee as she poured water into the cup, resulting in a droplet of the hot water dropping out of the cup and touching my tiny fingers. "Ouch," I said as quietly as I could. My aunt smiled and offered me her coffee to take a sip. I was exhilarated by the sip of coffee running in my veins and thanked her with the biggest smile I could offer. "Your smile is so big and takes up half of your face," she whispered while smiling back. I followed her to the kitchen's back door. She didn't like to smoke around me and managed to find a way to send me on an errand and out of her way for a little personal time.

Whenever she visited Iran, my family went to see her. She was a wealthy aunt who studied abroad and became a medical doctor. My grandmother and our relatives were proud of her. She was the talk of the party any chance her sisters had to brag about her to strangers and friends alike. She seemed to have it all from the outside: a medical doctorate with a romantic, tall, and dark-looking architect husband. Still, one thing my young mind could never understand growing up was the reason behind her smoking. "Does she enjoy it? Or is she sad?" I would ask my dad only for him to reply with, "Cigarettes are not good for your health." I never learned why, with everything in her possession, my aunt still sipped her coffee and puffed out smoke like an unfortunate poet all those afternoons.

It was only two years after my family immigrated to the US from Iran when I had my first. It was in college that I discovered smoking. My boyfriend smoked, and so did most of my friends. For about a year or so, I lived in a house with people who smoked something from tobacco to pot and occasionally other psychedelics. Somehow everybody managed to hold their jobs and finish up the schoolwork. Well, perhaps, except two people. One person decided to take a gap year from school, and the other one eventually left everything to start a rolling paper business in California. I never heard from them again.

As for myself, it was during that time that I learned about different ways my aunt might have felt. My first puff was both calming and exciting, a perfect bundle of a rolling roller coaster in rolled-up tobacco. After that puff, I felt that curtains were dropped from my mind, and suddenly I could understand and connect with my aunt. I could even read the meaning behind her gesture, leaning on the wall, profoundly staring to somewhere unknown, puffing her cigarette. In a way, on days I casually smoked a cigarette or two, my body language mimicked hers all those years ago. I knew for sure that my aunt was not fully happy.

Although short-term, cigarettes reduced my pain too and even helped me forget my loneliness in the world around me. I wanted to forget the pain of my loneliness, not having a solid support system, and not knowing what to do with my life. It was all on me to find my way, all alone. My parents brought me to this new country, and I was here, and it all felt as if I had fallen from the sky in an unknown land. It was around the same time in college when my style of having fun started to become unhealthy.

It was the last year of college, and my romantic relationship was on the verge of becoming non-existent after discovering my boyfriend had sent another girl flowers. I knew the girl. She was cute and flirty. When I confronted her, she told me she didn't know who sent the flowers. I was angry and wanted to scream, break, and destroy. I wanted to take it all out on him and serve him my best and strongest slap because he was supposed to be my rock. Instead, he was the running sand of never-ending drama. This time, he sent my favorite flowers to the girl I least liked.

Is he cheating on me? After all I did to help him with his school, let alone getting him accepted in the first place? Who does he think he is? I remember my head spinning with all those thoughts when I inhaled deeply from my burning cigarette. I felt the immediate rush of calm in my nervous system. As if I was hypnotized by the mix of extreme pain and intoxication, I focused my gaze intensely in the air and continued smoking just like my aunt. My broken heart was put to rest, and my mind was shut off. It was only the stream of cigarette smoke that seemed to exist, dance, and disappear into the same nothingness around me. It felt good and poetic, although unfortunate.

That night I ended up in the emergency room. My paperwork said that I was diagnosed with a nicotine overdose, a sporadic event, though, in my case, severe enough to keep me away from all smoky things for years to come. I sometimes wonder if my aunt ever went this deep into smoking herself. Then I remembered us, two small-town girls from the old world, roaming the vast grounds of the western world in Turkey and the US, miles away from our hometown. After that incident, I felt increasingly empathetic toward my aunt. I developed an unconditional love for her and the loneliness she might have felt all those years she seemed to live the glamorous life.

The isolation of this epidemic is kicking in hard; now I see the ghost of my aunt in my house. I rubbed my back. *Ugh, it hurts like hell.* I took another look at myself in the mirror. "You got this!" I said, affirming myself before clearing my mind with a deep breath. *I am healthy and happy today.* I hobbled back into the kitchen as the kettle was screaming at the top of its lungs with the news that it was time for coffee.

HOME

———

There is not much to say about life
It is merely a dream
A dream so vast
That gets me lost
In a fog-like memory.

I wrote in my notebook. Reflections and thoughts appear out of the blue and wiggle at the corner of my mind until I do something with them. To improve my ability to continue with my life, I've been keeping a journal on my desk for thoughts that emerge out of thin air. Writing calms my nerves, even when it is not perfect. This morning's short writing break was a brilliant match to my coffee. I haven't yet started the workday, but I feel productive already. I love being productive; it adds serious meaning to my life. Today, however, I was slower in my pace and perhaps more in a contemplative mood.

For an unknown reason, I wanted to pause everything in exchange for a bit of time to observe my surroundings. Looking around the room, the art supplies, a significant number of canvases, and both of my easels cramped up on the left corner of my living room grabbed my attention. Everything was piled up at the intersection of the kitchen and the narrow hallway to the bedroom. The whole scene of different-sized canvases laying against the wall gave that corner of my apartment a very artistic vibe.

The jumbled-up chaos ignited a thought. I got up from the chair and walked towards the bedroom. A great collection of books with colorful covers I had gathered over the years were neatly organized, like soldiers ready to march, on the floor by the window. In front of the book-soldiers was my queen bed, facing the east where the sun emerges each and every day. For a few moments, I thought of all the shit I've gathered over the years. The earthy and straightforward décor of the bedroom was giving it all the Zen vibes it deserved. *Does this Zen vibe mean that I am a balanced person too?* Just as the thought appeared in my mind, I realized a strange connection between the vibe of my room and my childhood home. Strangely, the way everything was arranged seemed to mirror the first home my family owned.

My family and I are from the historical region of Gorgan or Hyrcania. The name the city bears now, Gonbad-e Kavus, is a reference to an ancient monument within the city and means "the tower of Kavus." The tower is, in fact, the grave of Ziyarid ruler Kavus Ibn Vushmgir (r. 978-1012) and was built during his lifetime (Sherwin-White, 1993). The city itself is located in a region composed of the land southeast of the Caspian Sea in modern-day Iran and Turkmenistan and is bound in the south by the Alborz and the east by the Kopet Dag mountain ranges. The city's placement makes the area's climate generally hot and humid, with cold winters and warm summers.

The history of my region and its population goes back even further to the Neolithic period. The Jeitun culture was one of the early populations that started before 6000 BC in that area. Historically, Turkmen tribes lived a nomadic lifestyle and traveled by horse in a land without borders (*Encyclopedia Iranica*). My father told me once that the first Shah of Pahlavi, Reza Shah, ordered German civil engineers to redesign and build our modern city. "Perhaps he wanted to settle the nomadic tribes in the most important trading area northeast of Iran to protect the borders as allies," said my father.

For about four years of my childhood, we lived in the northern suburbs of Gonbad-e Kavus, across from the Gorgan River. The suburban area was near the horse-racing stadium, famous for holding races of elegant Turkmen horses. The site was called Yousef Abad, and it was under development when my family of five first moved there. Our house was a one-level single-family home on the north. When we moved into the space, constructions were still happening. Everywhere I looked, there were bags of cement, piles of sand, and construction materials. The entire living condition felt chaotic, as if there was no order to its madness.

As we were building the house and living in it, my parents constantly talked about their expansion plans for the home. They first worked with an architect to design a semi-modern family house with a gable roof. Because of their limited time and budget, they were only building half of their initial design. Their future expansion plan included one or two additional bedrooms on the east side of the building for my siblings and me to have more space. All my seven-year-old self wondered back then was when we would ever be done with all the construction so I could invite my friends over.

Similar to the US, it costs a fortune to build a family house from scratch. My parents were two teachers with a limited income and bigger dreams than their budget, so it was only natural that, initially, our house lacked many things, including an indoor bathroom. I remember having to go out of the house on cold winter days to shower or simply pee. On summer days, however, my siblings and I would shower butt naked under the sun. One day, we used up all the rainwater my parents had collected to store and use during the water supply shortage to play and shower in the yard. Water shortages happened so often, and our family desperately needed the supply. Once my father learned about what happened, he held me responsible for the situation. Without fully understanding the reason, I was yelled at and took a juicy slap on my cheek. In situations like that, I always ran away to my hiding spot, the attic, to cry and recover from the pain.

My father had a heavy hand, and he used it to punish his kids. His personal favorite was me. My sensitive and rebellious personality as a kid was out of the ordinary for my parents. Perhaps they did not know what to do with this small person with a gigantic disobedient soul. Even as a youth, I wanted everything to be done my way. My insisting on knowing the why behind everything was yet another peculiar trait for my family to deal with. On the other hand, the only reason I can imagine why he used physical punishments is that perhaps that was how his parents brought him up. Perhaps it was only the tradition that encouraged his hands to raise up in the air and come down on my body. Perhaps it was not his fault. It was common knowledge, however, that I was not alone in my upbringing. People did "that" to punish children who were not obedient. Through trial and error as an adult,

I have learned that is good to have some family than none. For that, I always prefer to return to the nest.

One other thing I know my dad managed to do a lot was build houses from scratch. While we lived in the first house under construction, almost every space undergoing construction seemed empty. The walls were colored either plaster-white or light brown. Because our home location was also under development and zoning, we were surrounded by empty fields where wildflowers grew for the first few years. I did not notice it back then, but open areas and earthy colors mean Zen and spiritual to me today.

Over the years, however, my parents managed to add more and more to the place. I vividly remember the day we finally could afford a landline in 1998. It took miles and miles of telephone cable cord for my dad to connect us to the central tower. *So bizarre and hilarious.* Mom, my five-year-old little sister, my three-year-old brother, and I were super excited about the phone when we called my grandmother to say hello for the first time. I still smile remembering the little family dance session we had in our kitchen out of excitement. Both of my parents liked to dance and for that we were the dancing family growing up. Happy from remembering the good moments of the past, I took a sip of the coffee I was holding in my hand while standing in the middle of my semi-empty bedroom. I was done time traveling in the past and finally it was time for me to head back to my desk.

It is so easy to work nowadays. I wake up and only commute the distance from the bed to my desk. I sit in front of the laptop that connects me with the entire team with only a few clicks. Within a few minutes of starting the workday, I was working, sending emails, updates, and pinging people on several platforms. My work demands multiple laptops and screens and often I switch between devices. It was about an hour later when I turned to my other work monitor that was idle. The screen was black, and I could see myself in it. As if I saw something out of the ordinary, this time, I gazed intensely into my reflection that was reminding me of the independent little girl I used to be.

Back when my family still lived in our Yousef Abad house, we all had to commute on dirt roads to get to the main highway to catch a taxi that took us to school or to buy a loaf of bread. My mother bought my siblings and me special shoes to help with the school trip when the roads got extremely muddy, especially on winter and rainy days. Some days, I would wear heavy-duty plastic bags to cover my shoes just to leave them behind if my feet got stuck in the mud. It took me about fifteen minutes to get to the highway from the house and catch a taxi every day.

On my way to school, my seven-year-old little figure would stand by the street and hold her hand to stop a taxi that would take her to school. *My parents seemed to have no fears about letting a seven-year-old catch a taxi to school all by herself. I cannot imagine a kid that young catching a cab by herself in Iran, nor in the US, nowadays. I was not a kid back then; I was a legit adult.* After school, I would walk back home with my friend and neighbor, Anna. In those days, most of us children commuted to school by ourselves.

Anna looked like Diana Barry, Anne Shirley's bosom friend and a kindred spirit in the *Anne of Green Gables* movie series. Her resemblance to Diana didn't end with Anna's appearance either, for they also had similar family dynamics. They both shared respected and friendly parents and one younger sibling. Our journey back home on foot would take us somewhere close to an hour if we decided not to take a taxi. Time flies when you are having fun, so the entire hour would feel short because she and I would talk about many things: our friends, our families, and art classes.

The entire hour-long walk back home with Anna felt terrific and, in a way, empowering. Together we crossed the Gorgan River, which was always muddy and brown. Sometimes the water would come up to the bridge, making it a scary scene. Other times, the river would look more like a rivulet. Together we would take out the mandatory headscarves and let the air rush into our hair. The first time we took off our scarves, I realized Anna's hair was light brown and was shiny and golden under the sun. "Oh, your hair is very black," said Anna, pointing her finger to my hair. We both laughed. The after-school walks with her were excellent and filled with strange conversations about eating wildflowers and painting pictures.

Anna and I commuted to and from school for a few more years. When I turned eleven, finally the construction was over, and our house was complete. My parents, however, did not like the location of our house and decided to move again: this time to another single-family house closer to the downtown and the historic Kavus tower. While it seemed logical to them, that decision was frustrating to me. I disliked the imposed change on my eleven-year-old self, who needed friends and peer validation more than ever. Right as I thought I could finally invite my friends over, we left the house, and I was once again friendless and alone. To this day, I never heard from Anna ever again.

I blinked at my reflection as I heard a notification go off on my laptop. I took another sip of my coffee and looked at the clock in the lower right corner of the computer screen. It showed 10:10 am. I had to get ready for my call in five minutes and started organizing the pile of colored notes in front of me.

SWALLOW BIRDS

———

My computer's clock showed 11:05 am as I turned my head up to look out of the kitchen window in front of me. A flock of birds was flying outside. With each turn, twist, and rise of their collective murmuration, my heart soared with the birds' movement, up and down. *I love these birds;* a fuzzy and warm feeling rushed into my chest and warmed my heart. For a moment, I felt connected with the flock of traveling birds. We had one thing in common—migration.

I have a faint memory of swallows from my childhood in Iran; I remember laying under the sun at my paternal grand-parents' terrace and imagining shapes out of the clouds when I saw a quick black bird with a strange tail descend in the sky. I asked my mother if the black bird was also a pigeon because many of them coo coo-ed in my grandmothers' trees. My mother told me that the bird I saw was a small bird called a swallow. "Although they are small in size," she added calmly, brushing my hair, "they are strong and can travel long dis-tances all around the world." My young mind wondered whether or not they took their family with them too.

It was the early afternoon of Thursday, May 27, 2010 when I was back at home from college, and our maid, carelessly, threw a bundle of letters inside from the doorway. Rays of afternoon sunlight were highlighting the bundle as I reached to see what is in the mail. Among all the other mail and a pile of advertisement cards, two larger, yellow-colored DHL envelopes attracted my attention. The handwriting on both was strangely awkward and seemed like a child trying to spell. Someone had written my name and address on one and my mother's on the other with poor Farsi writing. Both envelopes were posted from Kentucky, US, and had the Switzerland Embassy's stamp on them. Curious to see what was in the package, I opened mine.

To my surprise, I found a letter that was sent from the United States Department of State. I exhaled and held my hands in front of my mouth. My heartbeat started to run marathons, and I felt a cold chill run down the back of my neck and cover all my back. I took a breath. *Would it be possible? Did we finally win the Diversity Visa Lottery case?* I was anxious for more information while taking the letter out of its yellow envelope. I unfolded its creases and started reading.

The contents of the letter started with the following statement:

Dear GOLARA HAGHTALAB,

You are among those randomly selected for further processing in the Diversity Immigrant Visa program…

U.S. Department of State
Kentucky Consular Center
3505 North Highway 25W
Williamsburg KY 40769
U.S.A.

May 03, 2010

GOLARA HAGHTALAB
c/o NO909
KHAYYAM
FORODGAH
GONBADEKAVOOS, GOLESTAN 4971753968
IRAN

Dear GOLARA HAGHTALAB:

You are among those randomly selected for further processing in the Diversity Immigrant Visa program for the fiscal year 2011 (October 1, 2009 to September 30, 2011). Selection does not guarantee that you will receive a visa because the number of applicants selected is greater than the number of visas available. Please retain this letter and take it with you to your visa interview.

Approximately 100,000 individuals were registered for further processing. Therefore, it is most important that you carefully follow instructions to increase your chances of possible visa issuance. You must visit the Department of State website at dvselectee.state.gov where you will find instructions for completing the required processing steps.

Please be advised that your case may not be scheduled for an interview appointment until a visa number is available. You will only be contacted by the Kentucky Consular Center when a visa appointment is scheduled.

If it should be necessary to contact the Kentucky Consular Center, you must always refer to your name and case number exactly as they appear below. Your case number should be clearly written in the upper right hand corner of all documents and correspondence sent to the Kentucky Consular Center.

Case Number:
PA Name: HAGHTALAB, GOLARA
Preference Category: DV DIVERSITY
Foreign State Chargeability: IRAN
Post: ANKARA

The Kentucky Consular Center telephone number is 606-526-7500 (7:30am until 4:00pm EST), or send E-mail inquiry to KCCDV@state.gov

Even with my limited English, I immediately knew what the letter was about; we had won not only one but two opportunities of obtaining US green cards for our entire family. Completely excited and anxious, I called my parents. Over the phone, I could not explain the situation; my tongue was not turning well, and my parents were also not able to believe what they were hearing. However, if the letters were official and not a scam, they could provide us with an opportunity that could change the entire course of my middle-class family of five.

Immigrating to the US includes a long and expensive process. My dad was a bookworm, and Mom was a hardworking, ambitious woman, and still, our family did not have a significant amount of cash to pick everybody up and move them across the globe. For us, it was almost impossible to imagine the dream of living in the US becoming a reality. The incomes of both my working parents could not afford the expensive move. However, that day in May of 2010, I had the golden keys that could allow us to make the move with an affordable price tag within my hands. According to our research, all we needed to pay for was our health screening and travel costs to Ankara and the US. After a quick calculation, my parents thought that they could sell our house to help pay for our move across the globe.

Up until that day, we were, again, both living in and building our third house. This one was finally located downtown and behind the Kabus Ibn Voshmgir Tower. It was much bigger than the other two we had, with two business units attached to it. This house, with its modern and straightforward design, was my father's dream come true. When my family decided to immigrate, we were just done with construction, and it was time for us to invite our friends rtainment finally. But, two months later, in ldle East, and the old better life in the new became the migrating ut not every hundred ed aunts, uncles, cous-

e, such as one's voice, vocabulary, which she tely, immigration thor- dearest belongings and ntainer of herself with . Even now, many years of our decision to leave ld photos, and connect- hometown are the few of immigration. Unfor- not something I get to on me whenever I hear oming over for dinner or g assignments. itted my graduate-level g, he sent me an unhappy email recommending that I use an AI writing aid app that does spelling and grammar checks on my papers. For a hot second, I wanted to write back with an equally frustrated tone and tell him that I have a premium version of the app he is recommending and that I ran the writing through it multiple times before submitting it.

Although I did catch myself before sending the email and allowed a moment of pause to sit between myself and the so desired action, I did feel a rush of helplessness in my veins. *Fuck this!* A dreary sense of dark void started in my chest and spread all over my body before it swallowed my entire mind. *Goddamnit, R.I.P. my mental health.* So, I called my friend. When Marina picked up the phone, I whispered, "I knew I could not write well in English." Not only was my English not strong, but also, for the past ten years, I've been mourning the loss of my Farsi and Turkmen vocabulary.

All I remember from my native languages feels like a dream that faints day by day like a bird flying away in the sky until it becomes a faint dot on the horizon. Swallows, birds, airplanes, immigration, hell, and English were the words swirling in my mind when my thoughts finally got back to my chair in front of my work laptop and into my burning body. I was hot and had a headache. I wanted more coffee, while I knew water was what I needed. *I should stand up and take a break,* but I continued to sit on the chair. Finally, I felt alone in my frustration, my loneliness, my inability to write well in English and started a loud cry. I held my head between my hands, and I cried so hard, my lips felt numb.

Change is often inevitable and forces us to decide to let go of everything that is known and dear to us. Sometimes, by immigrating, we lose everything to gain more in life, but really, what did we achieve? Was it worth it? For all of us, migrants of the earth, deciding to leave our home country perhaps has been one of the most challenging decisions to make. Immigrating, for me at least, has been the most incredible leap of faith my family has ever taken.

For the former chatterbox that I was, losing my language and vocabulary was the first crease created on the mirror of my identity caused by immigration. In the early days, after we arrived in the US, I was feeling depressed because I could no longer talk or hold a normal conversation. After all, what was the point of talking when I could not express my feelings? Maybe one person could understand my feelings back then: the little mermaid from under the sea! But, as we all remember, she let go of her voice for a pair of legs to walk the path of opportunity.

I tried to take a long breath and another one after that until I was finally calmer. Getting up from my desk, I wiped my tears with my hands and went to get some water from the kitchen. My brain was working again, and I remembered the quote from the South African Author, GG Alcock, "We are usually unaware of our culture until we leave it and interact with people who are culturally different! This interaction and conflict raise aspects of our own culture to our conscious awareness! The irony is that the way we often find our culture is by leaving it!" In his book *Third World Child*, GG explains what happens to us immigrant kids.

Yes, it has been a hell of a journey. But let us face it, if I was still back home, I had to live a linear life and miss out on all the wonderful life experiences, European travels, my career, my first car, and the self-discovery that I have gained here in the US. So I felt a little grateful for my family's decision to leave Iran and drank the entire glass of water in one breath.

Just as I was indulging in thinking that my experience and struggles were unique, I thought of Ilnaz, a twenty-two-year-old Iranian-Turkish, and now an American immigrant: yet another swallow bird. I knew her family arrived in the US not long ago and decided to connect with her to see how she was doing. Because of the pandemic, Ilnaz and I bonded over a Zoom call, and she told me about Yalova, a small town in Turkey they lived in before coming to the US. The way she compared Iran, Turkey, and the US together was fascinating to me. Her story resonated with me in all the ways possible.

Before arriving in the US, Ilnaz was in the town of Yalova in Turkey. She was done with middle school recently and was studying as a sophomore in high school when her family decided to relocate to the US. Before Turkey, Ilnaz's family lived in my hometown, Gonbad-e Kavous. "How was Turkey?" I asked. "I was excited to move to Turkey. The cultural overlap helped with the transition process and made it much easier for me to find friends," she replied with excitement.

I knew from being in Ankara for about a month that the Turkish government and culture valued individualism and democracy more than Iran. At the same time, Turkish culture is still very much an old eastern culture that primarily values community. In that sense, Turkey still had a culture similar to the other eastern nations, including our home country. So, it was only natural for Ilnaz's alignment to the culture of Turkey to come quickly. But, on the other hand, her transition experience to the US was exceptionally different.

"US was not easy. Initially, I thought that there should not be much difference between the US and Turkey," said Ilnaz. "My friends in Turkey all had relatively pale skin colors. In my thoughts, that was like what I pictured America. Homogenous, Hollywood-like imagery of the US before arriving in this country. I was wrong." She took a deep breath. "What was the difference?" I asked my young friend. "When I first came to the US, I realized that this country was much more diverse than I first imagined. I met Asian, Indian, and Black populations who are not white." She continued by saying, "In the first days, I compared myself with white Americans because I truly thought they were real Americans and others were from different places and countries. You see, the race is not a topic of discussion back in Iran or even in Turkey, and my sixteen-year-old self was completely oblivious to it." I felt a cold sweat on my back. I remembered mentioning the same observation to a friend of mine for the first time. I understood Ilnaz wholeheartedly.

"Can you give me an example?" I asked again. She explained her story in almost one breath.

"One of my first experiences with race was when I had to check my race on an application form. I remember that selecting my race was super strange because I did not understand the race and even know my race. But, on the other hand, being put in a box based on my race seemed disrespectful to me. I only wanted to be Ilnaz from Turkey!" This time, I got chills all over my body. I remembered the first day in the US when I, too, had to select my race. The amount of confusion was overwhelming.

The most confusing part about our shared immigrant experience, however, was somewhere else. Both of us found it super strange that as soon as we shared our country of origin with people, their behavior would change. "Having people ask me where I am from and judge me was not an easy thing to deal with in my early days at school. Because of that, I started not to feel enough," Ilnaz shared.

Ilnaz continued explaining her feelings around the realization: "I felt unfit because I felt that who I am is not enough. I grew up in a family that loved me and made me feel enough. However, I was living in a community that looked like me and, from my perspective, were fellow human beings, but they were behaving in a way that made me feel not enough. I think as humans, there should not be differences among people. When I tried hard to fit in and copy other people's behavior, I lost my confidence in myself. As a result, I felt not enough for myself, so I decided to change the way things were."

Following our different paths, Ilnaz and I came to the same realization about ourselves that we are enough just the way we are. We didn't realize the path we were on as we went through it at different life stages. Now, however, we both can see how much we have changed and developed throughout the years. The good thing is that now we empathize with our younger versions of ourselves as we reflect.

As I was thinking about Ilnaz and her experience, I suddenly heard a loud noise caused by the birds outside, screaming and fighting over swimming in the puddle of water outside my window. Whether or not I was a great English writer, I had to re-do my paper again so there was no point in whining and complaining at this point. *I have come a long way so far, so I got this!* I patted myself on the back.

LANGUAGES

———

In the battle of languages
My mother tongue is fading.
and I am becoming a new multilingual me.

Again, I found myself writing and doodling in my notebook as I sat at my work desk under the bright mid-day light of my condo. *It is lovely here, and I am grateful for having everything I have now.* Birds were chirping, and Mort Garson's plant music playlist played as I recovered from the heavy lunch I just had. I felt like having Indian food today. By this point in time, my entire place smelled like the delicious vegetarian vindaloo. *Spicy food does things to me sometimes a man cannot do!* Just by thinking about it, my mouth watered. It was time for me to get back to work, but for some reason, I could not get my thoughts off the conversation I had with my boss earlier.

My manager, Abeo, is a thirty-some-year-old Nigerian American. His family immigrated to the US before he was born so they could continue their education. Today, we had a virtual coffee chat because he will be leaving our company soon. Our conversation covered all aspects of our work after his departure and the exciting opportunity at the new company. *I am excited about his next step.* As my discussion progressed with Abeo, I found myself speaking to him in all four languages I know to express my gratitude for his leadership and coaching. It felt as if English were not enough to share my sincerest feeling of appreciation for my boss as he moved on to his next adventure.

After all my degrees and life experiences in the US, I realized that my sense of being unequipped with words to express my thoughts and feelings persists. The English language lacks something for me when I want to have a heart-to-heart conversation with others. This realization sparked the idea of dedicating this story to language and culture differences I have experienced in the US and my home country, Iran.

One word that I wish to share fully and emotionally with people is "hello." Greeting others is a significant part of my culture as a Turkmen, Iranian, and Muslim woman. We value hospitality above all and love to provide a warm welcome to our guests and people we meet all the time. I like to think that hospitality is a virtue celebrated by many in the world. Even a tiny head nod on a walk could transfer a warmhearted feeling to someone who might be new in the neighborhood. I can imagine individuals worldwide nodding their heads or waving their hands to their neighbors while on a stroll. They might even say "hello" in more official and unofficial languages than I would ever know.

While "Hello," "*Salam,*" "*Dorood,*" and "*Merhaba*" are all united in their meanings, their uniqueness lies in the sacred background of the cultures and languages that house them. I am sure offering and receiving greetings feel much better when it is in one's first language. As for myself, however, I do not know of a single word that means hello in my mother's tongue, Turkmen. This reality, for me, leaves my greetings in other languages I speak emotionally unfulfilled, leaving me with a burning desire to say "hi" in a language that is close to my heart. However, I don't seem to find the word among the four languages I know: Turkmen, Farsi, Arabic, and English. As an Eastern Turkic person or Turkmen, my people hold a slightly different language and culture from western Turkic people in Turkey and Azerbaijan. People in Turkey use the term "*Merhaba*" to greet others. And guess what? The word, although it is labeled as an Ottoman Turkish word, has an Arabic origin. Ottoman Turkish borrowed extensively, in all aspects, from Arabic and Persian. Significantly, during the peak of Ottoman power (c. sixteenth century CE), words of foreign origin in Turkish literature in the Ottoman Empire heavily outnumbered native Turkish words, with Arabic and Persian vocabulary accounting for up to 88 percent of the Ottoman vocabulary in some texts (Center for Digital Humanities at Princeton).

Although I learned Arabic at school while growing up, since it was not a language I utilized at home, the word "*Merhaba*" didn't help me feel all fuzzy and warm in my chest. *Hmmm, Islam had a substantial impact on multiple languages in the middle east.* Unfortunately, as I pondered more on a word that could be the equivalent for "*Salam*" in Turkish before Islam, I found nothing to grab on.

Similarly, the Arabic word "*Salam*" also leaves me with a bit of a sense of separation when greeting others. Salam is heavily utilized and adapted in my second language, Farsi. This is because, like Turkey, Iran also adapted many Arabic words into its languages after Muslims invaded Persia. The Rashidun Caliphate carried out the Arab conquest of Iran from 633 to 654 AD. Muslim conquering of Persia led to the fall of the Sassanid Empire and the eventual decline of the Zoroastrian religion and language (*Encyclopedia Iranica*). Before Islam, the Persian word that meant "hello" was the ancient word of "*Dorood.*" While people still use it occasionally, it is not a word used in casual conversations by any means.

Compared to its Arabic versions utilized in Turkey and Iran, the word "hello" has lived a short time in the past thirty years of my life. I never had to use it growing up, except for English classes, and did not develop a feeling for the word. Because it is not attached to a dear memory from my past, the term does not carry nostalgia for me as an adult.

In my ancient and nomadic Turkmen culture, where its vocabulary holds no equivalent for the word "hello," our people use a one-word question to greet each other. "*Gowumy?*" is both a word and a sentence that implies care and welcoming at the same time for my people in Gonbad-e Qabus. I remember as a young person when my mother and her sisters would come together; they would ask each other if they were well or "*gowumy*?" The term translates to "*Nasil sin?*" in Western Turkish, "*Khoobi?*" in Farsi, and "*Kaif halak?*" in Arabic, and "How is it going?" in English. *Wow, this is fascinating even to me.* I took a deep breath and contemplated my natural complexity of holding multiple languages and cultures in one place.

As a result of thinking through such a complex topic, my body was physically in pain. *Ouch, I have to stretch.* As I stood up, my head hit the light bulb right on top of my desk. *Ouch! It hurts. This is what happens when I put my desk where it should belong to a dining table instead.* Once I got out of the desk area, I was already standing in front of the tall mirror.

I couldn't help but look at myself while stretching my back. It felt great to move a little. However, I couldn't help but look again intensely into the mirror.

As I looked into the mirror, my resemblance to my father's family jumped out at me. Like my aunt, I also had olive-brown skin, raven black hair, a pair of brown eyes, and a good figure. My smile that grows inch by inch into a full bloom whenever I smile reminded me of my second to last uncle's, but my lips looked just like my youngest uncle's, plump and pouty. I could hear myself talking to myself in English, and I remembered I have an unusual accent too. Even though I can speak English, I do not look nor sound like a white person. Suddenly, this observation that I am not white shook my body and trapped my breath in my chest. As if I was in a time travel machine, I started remembering the past.

My thoughts traveled back to August 12, 2017, where I was painting a mural in the corner at the University of Virginia in Charlottesville, Virginia. I was at the site earlier than everyone else and enjoyed the sunny day, my coffee, and the therapeutic task of painting. I immersed myself into my world so deep that it was only around noon when I became suspicious of no one else showing up at the site. *Where are all the other painters?* Regardless, I decided to continue working and ignore the strange fact. Finally, when I stepped out to get lunch, I realized no one was on the street either. Everywhere was radio silent, and even birds were not chirping. *Something is so off, G!* The realization hit my forehead when I saw chairs piled up in front of the store entrances. I decided to leave the alley I was working in and walk down the street, only to find out that all the stores were closed and secured with boards and chairs both inside and outside; at this point, I was panicked.

It was fear that ran my existence at that very moment as I realized I was alone in that abandoned corner. It felt as if I had walked out of my imaginary world into a war zone. With indescribable reflexes, I reached my pocket and felt my phone, pulling the device out with the speed of light. Something was telling me to check the news, so I searched for Charlottesville in the local news. There were live videos from the downtown mall streaming the brutal events that were happening. A woman was lying on the edge of the street in her blood. People were yelling, kicking, and screaming at the members of the white supremacists marching on the streets of Charlottesville. The air was heavy with violence, pain, and anger. My mind started swirling with thoughts both related and unrelated to the events I saw in the news. *Who would be the craziest yet bravest person who would pick me up in five minutes?* I had to get out of there.

Lucky for me, I had just the person to call: my friend, Iman, a tall, Asian-looking Turkmen young man who also happens to be from the same city as I am. I called Iman, and without any hesitation, he came to my rescue. The five minutes I waited for Iman passed like five years for me. From corner to corner, I struggled to find a spot to hide for my life because I was not a white person, had an accent, and certainly did not want to be murdered that day.

From the safety of Iman's car, I saw army tanks guarding the streets, and the city was going under a shutdown. Finally, we both made it home safely. But that day, for the first time, I became aware that people can and do get murdered in this country because of the color of their skin, their accents, or even their religion and culture. Even speaking a different language could be divisive and even dangerous in some places here in the US. I realized that I could be a victim of this collective hatred only because of my olive skin and accent. On August 12, 2017, what happened marked my first real experience with the history of race in America.

I could see the reflection of the oven clock in the mirror. *It is insane how our lives are bound by time.* I tried to shake the chills off myself. I took a spin on my heels, grabbed my ear pods from my desk and played, "This Is How It Goes" by Billy Talent, my favorite Canadian rock band, to clear my mind. *Sometimes there is no clear answer to explain the collective abhor that fills the world and walks the streets of the modern world still thirsty for blood.* I turned the volume up.

PART 2:

FEET ON THE GROUND

———

FASTEST GROWING
STARTUP

———

The main thing now is not to paint precociously but to be, or at least become, an individual. The art of mastering life is the prerequisite for all further forms of expression, whether they are paintings, sculptures, tragedies, or musical compositions.

PAUL KLEE

Is this my life? Sometimes I cannot believe it myself. The uncomfortable thought of whether I deserved my lifestyle and career bugged me as I worked away on a PowerPoint slide, completely forgetting the time. I was working on a client report document for rather some time. The work was bringing me joy and fulfillment. Suddenly, I grew a little taller, remembering the journey that got me to this point in my life. *I worked hard for everything ever since my first step here.* I paused and adjusted myself in the cashmere blend chair cushion. My eyes closed as I leaned back in the chair. I pulled out my hair tie and let the hair fall on my shoulders as I took a deep breath. My imagination took me on a flashback journey of the past twenty years from the suburbs of Yousef Abad to the United States' capital.

Ever since my thirtieth birthday, I have been feeling like a decent citizen. Finally, I am holding on to a job that is becoming my career and paying the bills like all the other adults around me. On top of that, these days, I find the career path I am on as a good fit for my personality. It is fun to be working for a leading international consulting firm. *My leadership team allows me to do a lot of things and explore.* My sister calls me Dora the Explorer primarily because of my haircut and sense of adventure. Large corporations allow me to grow and nourish the Dora inside me along with my sense of adventure. *Hmmm, and that feeds my yearning for constant learning and experimenting.* As I tried to think of my journey to date, my mind fogged up about the details, but I did manage to remember a mixture of feelings.

It was not clear what exactly I was feeling either. *Shit, this happens to me a lot.* Since arriving in this country, I was restless and frustrated most of the time. It felt as if all I have done was to put my entire energy into stretching my abilities to equal my peers. Suddenly, my memories marched in front of my eyes: the first place I worked at in Charlottesville's Fashion Square Mall, the jobs I left, the Piedmont Community College, my graduation day from Virginia, the life that has happened since then, the pains, the joyful days, and finally, this cashmere blend chair cushion and this career. I sat in my chair for a few more seconds, still unable to fully comprehend my feelings. *What just happened to me?*

Finally, I managed to focus and get back into my body. I was still sitting on my chair, so I turned my head up again and looked out of the window in front of me. There is an apartment building located across the street and down the hill. When it rains, the roof of this building houses puddles of water. I could see a few pools of water in there today; *it must have rained last night.* About twenty little birds were taking baths and making noises by the puddles. As I continued to watch them, I started repeating this sentence to myself in a low voice: "I am the fastest growing start-up." I cannot draw lines between the birds and what came to my mind about start-ups, but there I was, finally comprehending my thoughts—imagining myself as a start-up company! Something in me agreed with the statement.

In the US, we try to treat corporations as people. It is kind of funny that I was turning a person, myself, into a corporation. *Oh, you strange bird.* I giggled at my thoughts. With the same amusement caused by the idea, I got up from my desk and walked to the mirror by my dresser in the bedroom. I leaned in and looked at my reflection curiously. *Who the hell are you?* My image telepathically replied with, *"I am the fastest growing start-up."* I smiled with satisfaction.

The closest parallel I could draw between my commentary went back to when I first arrived in this country. At the time, I never had a job in my life before, nor knew how to hold one. However, I was the oldest in my family and couldn't sit at home to watch my father stress over money. For the first few days after arriving in America, my father's younger sister and I endured an hour bus ride and headed to the downtown mall looking for a job.

It was my first time at Charlottesville's historic downtown mall. It was a rainy day with a gray sky in November. The streets were wet and depressing. Even the woman in the café we first entered looked gray and sad. I felt as if I entered a new and unknown world of gray and pale humans. I asked the gray woman, who owned the café, if they were hiring. As a reply, she asked me a question. I didn't understand her question. Her speaking sounded like a bee buzzing in my ears, so I looked at her and smiled; she immediately dismissed us. My aunt and I didn't miss a single shop at the historic mall, asking if they were hiring. Shop by shop, we were rejected from them all. I felt as if I was trapped in a foggy town where all I knew about it was the bus stations with nowhere to go. I saw this unknown, cold, and gray land called Virginia and its gray people everywhere I looked. *It seemed better from the airplane!*

Despite being rejected from almost all the mediocre jobs I applied for, I could still feel a warm feeling deep down in my chest: a combination of wishful thinking and hopefulness that something better was on the way. Finally, only two weeks after we arrived in the US, I landed a job at Charlottesville's only indoor shopping mall. I was going to learn how to sell and repair watches. The twenty-one-year-old Golara in 2011 didn't understand any of her rights for working at a mall or a shop, so I agreed to get paid the smaller wage in exchange for a job that taught a skill. When I reflect on this attitude of mine, I realize how naïve I was back then.

Surrounded by watches of all kinds, I felt like I was in a wonderland where time was precious and even expensive. *Welcome to the USA.* I quickly learned to fix and repair watches. One week in, I was closing sales with my incredibly limited English. Two weeks into my job, I sold as many watches as possible and hit the highest sale record for the small shop. The store manager gave me a call to congratulate me. I couldn't speak English. Lucky for me, he was able to talk about it in a version of Farsi. Although his Farsi was not Iranian, we could still understand each other to a great extent. I felt accomplished. The ice-cold and gray image of my surroundings in this unknown land started to tremble. By hitting a high score on sales, I learned about achievement, the second most crucial element of the American culture. Time was expensive, and I was here to hustle and achieve everything I desired.

I started to feel proud that only two weeks after arriving in this new country, I had a job, and it was teaching me something. My broken English and strange attire didn't stop me from becoming one of the best sales agents at the shop. I was closing my sales in thousands. I was a good student and had a great teacher, my colleague—a twenty-two-year-old Afghan guy who arrived in the US as his third country, Khalid. He introduced me to his friends and helped with sales and English skills. Khalid even helped me study for my driver's license. Thanks to his excellent teaching skills, less than a month after arriving in the US, I passed the driver's license exam.

My second job in the US was a role at a high-end hair salon as a shampoo girl. On my off days, I would work on my third job as a hostess in an Indian restaurant. *I was crushing the blue-collar job market!* My weeks contained more than sixty working hours. My body would ache and hurt every night when I returned home, but I was on fire and swam in cash, or at least I thought I did.

Time was money, and I was cashing it. Because of the multiple jobs I had in the early years, my English improved rapidly. I made good money, and I spent most of it on clothing and high-end brands. When living at home, one can save a ton. I honestly thought I was doing alright for myself. Our family mentor, Ava, however, had other ideas about where else I could work. She, herself, primarily enjoyed writing and helping others. She was worldly and wise. "Your lifestyle is not sustainable. Now, you can work long hours on difficult jobs and have an income because you are young and healthy. In old age, these jobs will not serve you. I always tell my refugees that going back to school is a must for them. That is how you can thrive in this country," Ava said to me as we sat across from each other at a pizza place on the Barracks Road shopping center.

My family and I first met Ava at a local health center as we were finalizing our vaccines. It was only a few days after we arrived in the country. All five of us were at the center, sitting cheek to cheek, absolutely puzzled by everything. I do not remember how we got to the center. Whether or not we took a cab or someone gave us a ride remains unknown and foggy to me. All I know is that it was a cold day in December, and I do not remember struggling on the way to the health center. However, the way we got back to our apartment is crystal clear in my mind. We were leaving the center when a woman's voice called on us, "Do you guys need a ride?" We all turned toward the voice. She was standing next to a family van. Ava was tall and blond and was wearing a long, navy blue raincoat. "Did you come with IRC (International Rescue Committee)?" she asked again. I am not sure if it was myself or my dad who finally replied, "No, we came ourselves." Once again, Ava offered her van to take us home. I looked at my dad, and he at me, and then at all five of us. We got in Ava's van.

Ever since she has been part of our family, Ava became one of the reasons I am where I am today. My image moved in the mirror on my dresser from side to side, and my thoughts returned to my body. I was no longer traveling in the past, and my attention was back to the current moment again. I went back to my desk. As I sat on the chair, I placed my hand on my belly and took a few deep breaths. Doing this, I was immediately calmed. I sat there for a few minutes, thinking about nothing, allowing myself to only be in the present moment. Once fully relaxed, I could hear birds chirping outside. Some car's horn was going off. *Ugh, big city noises still annoy me.* The calmer I got, the better I listened to the world, moving into the future no matter what has happened in the past. I realized my sense of moving on too.

I turned to my laptop, put my hair in a bun, and started answering emails. The range of the email contents included everything from administrative issues to building foundations for emerging technologies. *I am impressed by how I understand this complex English writing, think critically, and offer potential planning and implementation ideas.* I was no longer entirely the girl who was looking for jobs at the mall in 2011. While I kept some of the core elements of who I was back then, I realized that my identity and life skills were expanded. One reason for my growth was understanding what I wanted and rejecting what I didn't like in work and life. The thought of my statement about knowing what I want once again sent me down memory lane.

It was in March 2012 when finally, I was invited to what seemed like an interview for a proper job at the University of Virginia. Ava was the one who arranged it. As I walked on UVA grounds, I could feel my heart beating in my chest. Deep down, I wanted more from this place than just a temporary job. At the time, however, I didn't know what I wanted from this university. I could only feel myself wanting more.

This was my first time visiting the UVA grounds, so I didn't know where things were or who I had to call for assistance. To be on time for my meeting, I decided to get there about an hour early. Finally, I found the building where I had my interview for a mail sorter job with trial and error. The redbrick building with a gable roof was located behind the physics building on the main UVA grounds. "Go around the back and ring the buzzer," said the gardener, who I stopped to ask for guidance. A few minutes later, I was standing in front of the back door of the building dressed in a gray coat and skirt from the thrift shop. I took a breath and rang the buzzer.

A woman's voice answered the doorbell. "I am here for an interview," I replied. When the door opened, I found myself in the basement of the building. It was terrifying! The rooms were dark with no windows, the vibe was matching the gray sky, my gray suit, and my heart was screaming "No!" I caught a glance of myself in the glass door of the mailing room as I walked in. The gray suit I was wearing was big for my tall and slim body. It was making me look more miserable than I was in that dark room. As I walked inside, I felt a heaviness on my chest. *Is this going to be my life in the US, the country of opportunities?* While I waited in the waiting room, an older woman with white hair and fair skin complimented my suit. "What brings you here?" she asked and went back into her office as soon as I replied with, "Work interview."

While waiting, I realized that every cell in my lean and slim body rejected the possibility of me working at this place. Terrified from the thought, I called our family mentor, Ava, on my cheap flip phone. "I don't think I can do this," I told her with a shaky voice over the phone as I looked out of the basement's only window that showed nothing other than flower bed dirt. As if she felt my emotions, Ava responded with, "Then leave the place!" I was shocked for a moment and replied, "Do you really think I can do that?" She replied calmly, "Absolutely!" I stood there for a second, unable to internalize the permission I was just given to do what I thought was best for me.

Finally, as if something warm wrapped around my body, I felt courageous enough to walk out. Without even telling the receptionist that I was not interested in the position, I walked out of the building. As soon as I was out of that place, I felt free. My spirit expanded to match the greatness of the blue sky, and the sun started shining again! Although I never worked at that mailing room to sort the mail, I did end up at UVA only two years later. I was there with an entirely different purpose: to study and be a student!

Suddenly, I was right back to the present moment as I heard my notifications go off. My colleagues were looking for me. Once I was aware of my body again, I found myself starring at the rooftop of the building in front of me with no birds bathing anymore. The sun was shining, and I put my glasses right back on and turned my face toward my work laptop. *I love working, and I do not mind being a fast-growing start-up.* A smile filled my face, and I paused to write on my notebook:

The road keeps me moving curiously
I am grateful for its winding curves
Housing glory
In all hidden corners
Every breeze I meet on the way
Whispers in my ears
Be brave!

WHAT ABOUT FUN?

———

I wonder what happens to my body when having fun. In most cases, every piece of my body loosens up. I become lighthearted, smile a ton, and act silly. Creativity blossoms in every action, in every thought, and my spirit lets her mental guards down. Earlier today, thinking about having fun boosted my energy, I felt warm inside. While sitting on my chair, I looked over the stacks of books on my desk in front of me. Almost all of them covered topics around the use of self, organization design and workforce development. *What are these books trying to tell me? How can anything other than quick video demos be absorbed more accessible by people in the era of Google engine searches? Will adding fun help? How can I do that for my team while I am new to the US and corporate culture myself? Fun means different things in different places.* I held my head between my hands and gently rubbed my forehead.

While juggling all these questions in my mind, I remembered my team's "No Judgment" video calls. We decided to have no structure or agenda for these calls. The goal was to connect and have fun. Since working virtually isolates, as a team, we found value in simple gatherings. People were encouraged to show up just how they are with their kids and pets on the screen or in the background. We shared, laughed, educated, and showed off our house plants and puppies so others could enjoy them too. Each time we gathered as a team without an agenda, everyone's vibe was relaxed with their guards down.

In 2018, I decided to commit to the idea of work as play to stay creative and fulfilled. Back then, I worked for a strange, progressive lab at the University of Virginia. The Make to Learn Lab was part of the school of education and human development. The co-directors of the Lab were two professors: one specialized in communication and the other in mathematics. While their skills were complementary to each other in most cases, they both shared a keen desire for adding the element of fun to their work with students. Designing games was their solution for adding joy and laugher everywhere in the educational curriculums. I was hired as an artist in residence who helped design engaging curriculums for K-12 and college students. My daily work, combined with a dose of fun, enabled me to become an empowered version of myself; a more potent, unapologetically creative, solid, and refined version of myself I never knew I wanted to become.

I do not consider myself the best student, but I was both the best student and the best teacher I ever was in my life at the Make to Learn Lab. In many ways, the fun and creativity I encountered at the lab enabled me to tap into many dimensions of my being, one of which was my femininity. Every day, I showed up sporting a long and flowy skirt to build speakers and motors. The contrast of my femininity within a masculine environment was the right amount of boldness I craved in my life. The yin and yang in me were balanced for the entire time I worked at the lab, submerging myself to the point where art and science came together.

We incorporated toys, music instruments, crafts, drawing, painting, and language arts into the curriculums for engineering and science classes. Once the animation was created, we encouraged K-12 and college students to turn their animation machine into an automated version by adding codes. For example, to teach students programming, we would ask them to read a fictional book. After, they had to pick one story and turn it into segmented drawings. Using cardboard, 3D printing, mirrors, simple motors, and design elements would add movement to their sketches. By this point, they would master simple algebra. The simple algebra they learned up to this point would help them map out the code they needed for automating their devices.

One summer afternoon, one of the directors and I talked about work-life balance when he said: "We are here to play and have fun at the Make to Learn Lab!" His statement, accompanied with a mischievous smile of his, kind of stuck with me that day. *Maybe he turned on a light bulb in me that already existed?* I was not sure. Ever since that interaction, I am constantly looking for opportunities to turn my work into a fun and engaging activity. The "No Judgment" video calls these days serve the same purpose, allowing my team to have the foundation needed for fun to happen.

Our casual team environment in the past year has allowed me to get to know my colleagues better. Sophia is an American-born Italian woman with dark, long hair and hazel eyes. She is friendly, independent, professional, and fun. Every day, I learn something incredible from her about work because she often knows the best way to execute ideas is to toy with them until the best outcome is achieved. While her powerful execution skills are immediately recognized, I also appreciate Sophia's mastery in thinking and communicating clearly at work. *She has a crystal-clear mind;* I wonder how she does it. It is only natural for me to wonder about the reason behind her ability to be laser-focused in all areas of her professional life. *Is she the same way in other dimensions of her personal life?* As for bringing joy and fun to work, she has been the most productive among all of us.

The other day, Sophia invited me to join her and her husband for dinner. Happy to spend more time with them and curious to get to know her better, I accepted. "She attended an all-women high school, you know, and her friends from that school are all like her, independent and smart," Ian, Sophia's husband, explained. "What you see in her is precisely the reason I was attracted to her in the first place," Ian added. *Wow, an avant-garde woman.* I had nothing else to ask; Sophia seemed fun, exciting, brilliant, and innovative both at work and in her personal life. What else was there for her to accomplish? I did not dig deeper.

If it were not for our team's fun and relaxed working style, I would not get to know Sophia and her husband. Perhaps we would be working in our separate worlds and never become aware of the talent and stories of others. While still sitting on my chair, I decided to grab *Your Unique Cultural Lens* by Enrique Zaldivar from the pile of books next to me. While slowly flipping through the pages, I tried to think of my cultural lens that might have contributed to the judgment I had of Sophia as someone unusual. *I am coming from a culture where women are mostly suppressed. It is natural for me to recognize a strong and outspoken woman and be astonished by her.* I realized that my background experiences were leaking into my professional life. *What else passes through these two worlds?* I wondered.

Perhaps my yearnings pass back and forth between personal and professional lives. I might be looking to fill a gap in my personal life by working a lot or wanting to have a piece of my personal life's comfort at work. I realized that perhaps my desire to play with ideas and have fun at work could have a deeper reason. *Damn, this is exciting, AND thinking like this gets real exhausting quickly. It is time for a five-minute break.* I got up from the chair and stretched my elbows and back. *Uh, stretching feels good.*

While the Make to Learn Lab was where I experienced firsthand the benefit of play, when I investigated the idea that work should be fun, I realized that idea came from my childhood. *Of course!* Back in Iran, when I was only seven years old, our neighborhood was buzzing with many families and their children. Among them, there was an older girl with impressive creative talent. Her name was Hamideh. Her name means "praiseworthy" in Arabic, and indeed Hamideh lived up to her name. Initially, she taught me to play and have fun even when I had to do chores. Hamideh herself would do everything creatively, which is why she felt free, happy, and expressive.

Since her family was traditional, she had to wear a headscarf as soon as she turned nine years old. That is the age Muslim girls are believed to reach puberty. I remember her innocent smile as she tied her scarf on her chin. Every day she would sweep their humble house with a natural corn broom, take care of her little brother, and stand in a long line to get fresh bread for her family without ever complaining. She would turn a task in her hand into something that she could enjoy and have fun with, whether cleaning the house and helping with the chores around the kitchen or watching kids younger than her. Hamideh kept her creativity with her all the time, and it was all her humble soul had.

I always envied her skillful artistic talent. I would often find her sketching, stuffing the new doll she built, or stitching a doll cloth she just designed and cut a moment ago as she babysat for us. After she was done with her work, she would gather us children around and have us talk about her sketches or play with her dolls. One day, she sketched drawings of my sister and me and told me that we were in a story. I remember disagreeing with her over something that happened in the story she was telling us, but she laughed and laughed. My feelings inspired me to start sketching, creating dolls, and come up with ideas to play with. I think Hamideh taught me to connect the day-to-day life with something I sincerely enjoyed. Although I do not believe I've fully embraced the idea of fun at any given moment, the desire to play and have fun always shows up when I am at work.

I grew up with the repeated theme of work as play, and it only took twenty years when Professor Bull at UVA School of Education reignited the idea in me and helped me strengthen the flame. One day, he told me that coming to work for him is like going on a playdate with colleagues. "You too can have a career that will allow you to have fun and play," he declared. Without knowing, his statement became one of my central values to date. When applying for a job, I want the company's environment to allow me to play and co-create with others because I believe that our happiness drives the way we show up at work and even in life. *I am glad for the team I work with now.* My teammates help me get closer to my ideal of work as play and live a more balanced life. Just the right amount of *yin and yang!* I shifted in my seat, reaching for the glass next to me for water. It was empty. *Uh, an opportunity to stand up and walk for a minute.* I smiled at my positive thinking and got up to get water.

THE GHOST

———

I was looking out of the window while lying on the pink velvet couch in my living room. "Beep, beep, beep." It was the notification sound going off on my work laptop across the room. *Ugh, here I am being recalled again.* So I finished the rest of my water, got up, and walked to my desk. I had a ping from my boss. "Do you have a second to talk?" I stood there for a minute, feeling anxious and terrified. A thousand dark shadows of uncomfortable thoughts rushed into my mind leaving me worried to the point that I started visibly shaking. My mind went to the worst possible ideas. *He will ask me to roll out of the project or tell me that a comment I made was wrong and inappropriate. Jeez, what if I said something that came across as weird without even knowing?* The thoughts spiraled in my mind with no end to them. Finally, I replied to my boss's question with, "Sure, how can I help?" Interestingly enough, what he had on his mind had nothing to do with me or my performance. He wanted to talk about a challenge of his own and needed a soundboard.

It is only recently that I learned to pause whenever I feel anxious for no valid reason. Fifty-five hundred minutes of meditation later, since this past January, I can now recognize when and how to disengage from my thoughts. When I pause to question my feelings, I hear the tiny little sound in my mind that usually reminds me of my hard work and incredible work ethic. Where I used to sit with massive self-doubt, now I sit presently, remembering that at this very moment, nothing is threatening the little Golara. The journey to this self-awareness, however, has been a challenging one all along. The hardest part for me was acknowledging the times the ghost of anxiety emerged from the shadows.

I remember calling her a friend, the woman who said to me, "I have seen your ups, and I have seen your downs and do not think you will get anywhere in life," ruthlessly. Something in me knew she was false in imagining her abilities to read my future. That night, I decided not to be like her, a friend who doesn't know friendship. One more thing that emerged from the darkest parts of my subconscious from that interaction was the ghost of anxiety. *Nice to meet you,* I said to the irregular heartbeat mixed with a small dose of panic attacks; *I didn't know a ghost lived under my skin.* As I sat on the sofa and listened to that woman's comments about my future, I sensed the spirit growing bigger than myself. In a matter of moments, her entire house became darker in energy. All I could see was her lips moving. *I will never call you my friend.* I managed to find a polite reason to leave her house forever.

Sometimes I feel the ghost walking shoulder to shoulder with me. It shows up when I'm interacting with others; it disappears for the most part when I am alone. I know that it is never wholly gone, more like it becomes invisible. The ghost is less visible when I am around others I have known for a very long time or talk to people with the same ethnicity, culture, or country of origin as myself. However, there are times in my life where the ghost becomes almost as prominent as myself. Often, I feel its strength when I'm talking or interacting with people who are different from me, let it be in mindset, spiritually, or based on their location and culture. Since I moved to the US, I find it difficult to assimilate with people's cultures in this country. Most of my cultural belief seems to be almost on the opposite side of the stick compared to most people here, which stresses me.

A few weeks after we arrived in the US, my colleague at the watch place who lived next door offered to give me rides to work. I didn't know how to respond to his kind offer. On the one hand, my family still didn't have a car, and it took me an hour to get to work by bus. A car ride would have shortened the travel time to only a few minutes. On the other hand, he was a young and unmarried man. In my culture, a good woman, especially if she is young, doesn't get into such a person's car alone. If the situation was not preventable, I was taught to take the car's back seat. After much thinking, I decided that it was only logical to drive with my colleague who lived in my neighborhood.

I remember it being a stressful morning. He showed up at our door with his car's speakers blasting music I was not familiar with even a bit. I wanted the earth to open up so I could get in there and disappear. Maybe at my core, I didn't want to get into his car, but I didn't know how to avoid it properly. It didn't help my situation even a bit due to the fact that he also was a handsome man. *My people would assume something romantic is going on.* I didn't want them to think that way at all when all I needed was a freaking ride to work.

"I am a good woman," I said to myself quietly. With sweaty palms and full-on anxiety, I decided that it would be impolite not to get into his car now that he was parked in front of our apartment. With a short hesitation, I opened the back door, got in, and sat politely. "Hi," I said awkwardly and added, "Thank you for…" I was not done with my sentence when he looked back at me with visible confusion on his face. "Hmmm… I am not your chauffeur, Golara!" And then he added, "I thought we could be friends." At this point, I didn't know what the hell to say. My anxiety bubbled in my chest and then spread to all of my body. Its energy circulated everywhere, leaving me light-headed and dizzy right before disappearing. Finally, the energy materialized into a darker, dimmer representation of myself, sitting next to me on the car's leather seat.

"Hmmm, what do you mean?" I replied to his question anxiously. "Why are you sitting in the back seat? Come and sit in the front. We are going to listen to some dope music," he said. *What on earth does "dope" mean?* As I got out of the car to move to the front seat, something told me that my uncle-in-law would see me sitting in this car with a strange man. The ghost grew in size. I continued imagining my uncle reporting back to my parents about my extremely reckless behavior that jeopardized the family's reputation. I was terrified, and my mouth was dry as I decided to get back in the car and sit in the front. Later, I found out that my uncle did see me sitting in the front seat of a "random" young man's car listening to some dope music. Perhaps my carefree vibes didn't sit well with the uncle's honor that morning. When I was back from work, my parents had some questions for me. My ghost again grew more extensive than my physical body and sat next to me at the kitchen table that evening as my parents recited the entire list of good woman mannerisms.

Most of the time, the differences between American culture and my version of traditional culture show up almost as an imbalance in values. For example, a good woman in my culture is always polite and does not engage in behaviors like dating and having premarital sex or even simply making eye contact with a man. Because of the internal conflict caused by the differences I encountered in my earlier days in the US, I lived in a constant agony between not knowing what I am allowed to think, do, or say and when I should let go in different situations. For the past few years, I held hands with the ghost who sat next to me at all times. *Phew, again, my thinking is getting too tangled in different topics. I need a break.* I tried to channel my concentration back to work.

It took me a few minutes before I was back to thinking about the source of my inner conflict. *I can only point out that I am an immigrant from the old world.* Sometimes I think that perhaps I traveled in time. I remembered reading a paper written by Professor Ronald Skeldon, a professorial fellow at the School of Global Studies at the University of Sussex, published in the World Migration Report 2020 on "Rethinking International Migration." He mentioned that "migration is the most problematic of the population variables that are taken as given. Unlike the unique birth and death events that define an individual's lifetime, migration can be multiple events. Its measurement depends entirely upon how it is defined in time and across space." The difference in culture between where I am coming from, and the mechanical culture of the US machine is not limited to day-to-day interactions but also an indicator of everything that has happened throughout their separate histories. By this point, my thoughts were exhausting. I walked up to the large window in the living room and looked out at the trees in the distance and took a deep breath.

I have done everything I could in the past years to learn about the culture of America; I turned my back to the window.

I can still detect my obliviousness toward its different layers, Goddamnit! I was frustrated that my multicultural background was causing me anxiety. To help solve my little ghost problem, I did what I do best at times of ambiguity and became curious about the ghost. While searching for resolution, the nature of my community and the people in the US popped out to me. The old world was collectivist and community based while in the US, people are more individualist. *My upbringing in a tribal-based world may be why everything in the US seems to sit on the opposite end of my views.* I crossed my arms over my chest and pondered.

In his book about culture and organizations, Geert Hofstede defines collectivist societies in which the group's interest prevails over the interest of the individual. On the other hand, a society in which the individual's interest prevails over the group's interest is called individualist. My upbringing mainly concentrates on being a good woman for the good of everybody in my family, which means the honor of everyone is bound to the honor of their women. In many ways, it is also correct that the definition of this good woman is similar to what was defined in 1950s America or in earlier times and in the way European societies expected a woman to act in Regency era England. *What do you think, Golara? Are you a good woman or a bad one?* I marched towards the kitchen, then to the bedroom, and back to the living room. My mind wanted to explode.

There are few commonalities to pinpoint when drawing parallels between my culture and the American understanding of a good woman. Based on my first culture, a good woman is agreeable, talks slowly and calmly, and never uses curse words. *Well, I use swear words here and there.* She even walks and dresses appropriately; *I got this one, though.*

Growing up, it was ingrained in me to avoid behaviors such as keeping eye contact with people or greeting and befriending single men. At the same time, my peers in the US were educated that their assertive, confident nature is respected as a woman. My peers were empowered to think critically when looking for a solution to a problem and ask all sorts of questions. The Me Too movement and other woman empowerment initiatives encourage American women to love and respect their bodies however way they want.

While my original culture has many attributes for being a good and godly woman, I believe it is now time for me to find the middle ground between the spectrum of individualistic and collectivist societies; something that works for me and the person I am. *I now am a part of both, so I better start learning how to deal with it.* As for people's judgment, especially those with the same background as mine, I decided that their judgment is only a reflection of who they are as a person. While being aware of my growing anxiety, I decided that finally, it was time to experiment.

RACIAL EDUCATION

———

I was just done taking the last bite of my post-lunch mini burrito when I received a message on my grad school cohort's channel. One of my classmates shared a link to the podcast mentioned during our class last weekend when discussing multiple social justice issues, including racism. I clicked on the link, and it took me to the *Good Ancestor Podcast* by Layla F. Saad. Layla's smiling image on the home page with a black headscarf, pink lips, and wearing an elegant blue top immediately sent me down the memory lane in my journey on racism.

I had a terrible headache as I walked down the streets of Columbia Heights neighborhood in Washington, DC. The chilly breeze of October weather was only adding to my pain as I passed by a group of Black women. Almost immediately, I found their perfume extremely disturbing. My headache got worse, and I felt nausea. "Their cheap perfume is making me feel sick," I blurted out to my then fiancé as we walked together. "You are a racist," he said. *Shit! These were the words of a man to who I was about to devote the rest of my life.* I stopped walking and started listening. "What do you mean?"

I asked. He had no real explanation; instead, he just left me and never came back.

After he decided to break up with me, I spent about two months living in agony and shame, thinking I was the problem. My thoughts went as far as even thinking that he might be true and that I am a racist person. But, eventually, as if an internal light bulb turned on, I became determined to change that status about myself. The first realization that came to me was that I did not fully understand race in America. So, with hopes of finding ways to help me grow out of my obliviousness, I knocked on many doors both literally and metaphorically.

Fortunately, one of the doors that opened up to me was the opportunity to enroll in the Master of Science in Organization Development (MSOD) program at the American University (AU). The program promised to help me increase my self-awareness and knowledge of systematic social and human issues. *Learning about different systems in the US would definitely help with the understanding race too.* I was sold on pursuing it almost immediately. Our cohort began the program in January of 2020. While the decision of going back to school for personal growth was obvious, I still could not determine the complete picture of the desired outcomes I wished to cultivate during my time at AU. All I cared to undo was the "racist" label put on myself.

I saw the significant impact of my obliviousness around race pretty soon after enrolling in the MSOD program. During the first couple of sessions spent with the cohort, I made a statement about skin color. To share the extent of my initial obliviousness around race, I will share the exact sentence here. During our second session with the cohort, I landed on the topic of race with a sentence that started with

"I do not see color!" An excellent "wow" filled the room, and everyone held their palms in front of their wide-open mouths. Not knowing what I did wrong, faced with the reaction, I started crying.

What I thought I meant at that time was that I see everyone as equals. Later I was told that members of white supremacists frequently use this very sentence to justify their behaviors. Again, I was ashamed, afraid, and despairing because of what I said, this time in front of about twenty people. While it was challenging to be "that person" among my cohort from the get-go, I was still determined to get educated on the topic until I could feel the struggles and pain of Black people as mine. I continued to feel slightly threatened for days because I thought no one in the cohort would like or respect me anymore. Observing everyone's reaction to my statement, I was face to face with my eternal fear of not being liked by others. This feeling stayed with me until one day, Tiff, a Black woman in our cohort, sat next to me. "They will give you grace," Tiff said, looking me in the eyes. I didn't know what to say or feel other than being eternally grateful for her.

During the virtual Use-of-Self Residency, I was able to discover my connection to others with marginalized backgrounds. Our cohort was gathered for a highly experiential course offered by the program during this week-long intensive retreat to build skills and self-awareness relevant to working with diverse individuals, small groups, and large organizations. From the get-go, each of us was assigned to a Learning Support Group to discuss the topics mentioned in the class. One of the topics contained issues around race. During these discussions, I was finally able to share my frustration around figuring out my placement and identity on the racial grid of America. The Learning Support Group included a white gay man, a Black straight man, and three straight Black women. As a group, we made sure to indulge ourselves in topics of race, identity, and immigration for the entire time we had together.

Luckily, in my group, we discussed race in America in detail. The safety I experienced during these discussions helped me learn about Black lives and draw connections to my background to build context for myself. *I wanted to feel their feelings and be with them in their pain.* When I shared my frustration around my skin color, the group listened and allowed me a safe space to unveil my inner thoughts to them. "Although my skin color is tan and I do not look white, US Census identifies me as a white person," I shared with the group. I could see raised eyebrows even in the virtual room. I continued my sharing by saying, "Regardless of who the Census thinks I am, there have been times that I was not treated as a white person in the US because of my skin color." Then, I lowered my voice, "I do think that I too carry ignorance towards race caused by the absence of context as a recent immigrant," I added. More eyebrows were raised in the room. "This whole thing is very confusing to me because of many opposing facts," I shared with the group, frustrated, and added, "My Iranian upbringing did not include any acknowledgment of race. All we had was ethnic groups and wars between them," I concluded. For a long minute or so, the room was silenced.

Finally, one of the Black women in the room broke the silence. *It is always a Black woman who rescues me from awkward moments.* "I hear you, Golara. A few years ago, I traveled in Asia and didn't understand a single word in their language. The first few days without a translator felt strange as if I was lost," said Char. I appreciated her sharing a lot that day because it enabled me to connect with her and my other Black classmates. To dig deeper and investigate my experience on the topics discussed above, I decided to create a side-by-side table that laid out the subjective and objective data that existed in the initial state of my experience (Patwell, Seashore, 2006). According to the American-Austrian sociologist Peter L. Berger, things unseen to the individual are subjective and can become objective once the person becomes aware of their reality.

Inward Observation of Self (subjective)	Outward Observation of Self (objective)
I was called racist by my ex.	I was being judged.
I believed him when he called me a racist.	I was showing up with a low self-esteem level.
I decided to learn about race.	I enrolled in a master's program that studied systems and human behaviors
I made a racist comment publicly.	I performed without genuinely thinking or feeling about the impact I could have on others (Yeganeh and Kolb, 2009).

After I finished writing my table and contemplating my behavior, I now realize that I was initially unaware of myself and my reactions. As a result, I was subject to the events that were happening around me. My unawareness caused others to blame me, which resulted in elevating my state of being into the aware zone. This change, although painful, helped me become more accountable with my behaviors. When imagining the ideal future state for myself and learning more about race in America, I realized that I needed to clearly understand my actions and self to build meaningful relationships with a diverse group of people (Kegan and Lahey, 2001). This seemed to be the only way I could fully develop into a person who could understand others.

Reevaluation of where I am translates to an action that calls for building my emotional intelligence. *Bitch, you are up to something here.* Developing my emotional competency that includes both aspects of self-awareness and self-management was the key to my transformation. *This got deep again. Deep thinking leaves me so hungry.* I went to the kitchen to see if there was anything left for me to eat. The only thing I could find in the refrigerator was some leftover hummus and carrots. I gobbled it up with the speed of light.

In addition to my learning throughout the MSOD program, my self-awareness increased tremendously because of my daily meditation practices. It has been closer to a year since I completed the Mindfulness-based Stress Reduction (MBSR) course; yet another attempt of mine toward self-discovery and awareness. *I was so tired of being a basic bitch.* The MBSR course is created at the University of Massachusetts (UMASS) by Jon Kabat-Zinn, PhD. It is an eight-week program that provides secular, intensive mindfulness training to help individuals with stress, anxiety, depression, and pain.

Oh boy! I thought, *to have all of the above when I attended the first session back then.* Many moons later, and while having a daily practice of my own, I have now started to see the impact of my mindful living on raising the self-awareness I gravely desired back in 2019, although I still feel weird most of the time when it comes to an understanding my surroundings.

Now my ex symbolizes an omen, as Paulo Coelho talks about in his book *The Alchemist. Wow, I am grateful for that man; he was yet another sign from the universe for me to wake up and grow.* I was thankful for him, for my journey, and my Black classmates for helping me understand. *To be able to understand is to be able to love.* I closed my eyes and took a deep breath. Once I opened my eyes again, I thought of all Black men and women who helped me in my journey, and my heart became filled with gratitude. I pressed play on Layla's latest interview with a Pakistani-American artist and activist.

COMPASSION

———

Growing up, I was not the most grateful or compassionate person in my family. Even as a young adult, I was not the kindest person around. My friends were few, I lived in my head, and my tongue was sharp. I was quick to state the obvious and brutally shared the truth everywhere I went. But things changed in 2019. I endured a pivotal moment in my life.

I feel like love stories are kind of the same everywhere. I want to say I am unique with what happened between me and my ex, leading to this pivotal moment of self-realization, but I would be lying. Breakups happen to many people, and almost all of them hurt at least a little. What happened to me was that one person's behavior upset me just enough, so that I became encouraged to change my behavior and with that, myself. *Now it sounds like I experienced trauma. Maybe I should explore that trauma.* I was struggling with my thoughts when the world around me trembled. The ground under my feet cracked. I found myself in a moment in time where I was sitting behind my car wheel in Columbia Heights, DC. It was a warm and sunny afternoon of November 2, 2019.

"I am afraid I cannot provide you with financial support. I also find you very harsh, Golara." His last two sentences spiraled in my head. My ex-fiancé was an editor at a prominent and internationally known news agency. His father was a highly respected medical school researcher and a surgeon. His mother, although she had obtained her medical degree, decided to become a housewife. And he thought I, an artist who just recently changed career paths with no significant reserved cash was going to be a financial burden for him and his family. *Maybe they thought I was a gold digger!* I found even the thought of it nauseating. *If anything, my highly motivated and ambitious ass would add more money to their family.* I sighed and placed my head on the steering wheel. Deep down, I knew there was more to me than the shaky, tiny piece of shit sitting in that car! For the moment, however, I felt ashamed.

I was ashamed of my parents, my family in Iran, friends, and even never known strangers as I drove on the DC streets. I was ashamed of the called-off wedding, and I blamed myself. *If only I were kinder. Suppose my tongue was not as sharp. If only I were less of myself, maybe I could get married.* I think both in my culture and worldwide, marriage for a woman still equals a high honor. For some reason, if we don't have that one certificate in our tote of accomplishments, we are not entirely successful. So, it was only natural that I wanted to change myself to fit the bill at that moment.

With all the pain and the madness I was going through internally, I sensed a tiny amount of warmth at the bottom of my broken heart. For some reason, I thought that I was walking down the right path. Regardless of me getting married or not, something had to change about me. I was not sure exactly what that was going to be. It is easy to say couples can learn and grow together. With my ex gone, the growing part was on me. That day, I vowed to become the kindest and wealthiest woman I could ever become. I was not sure how to gain financial abundance just yet, but I knew then that I had to start with loving myself to become kinder.

It might sound simple to pick it all back up and love yourself. The truth is that self-love is not easy. At first, I had to face my fears and then my imperfections. I had to come out of my head and step out of myself to look back at the person that I have been all these years. I decided to gamble and take a leap of faith. The same night, I emailed someone I knew who maybe could help. At least he knew more than me about mindfulness and meditation practices. I also hoped he knew about resources in the DC area. Lucky for me, he replied with a long list of recommendations two days after I hit send on the strangest email I ever sent someone I barely knew. I now had a plan.

If I read these ten books he recommended, I will become a better person. This was only wishful thinking and the journey had more to offer than an easy exit. Each book I read opened a wound in me I didn't know I carried. One mindfulness-related book after another, I learned about my shortcomings in communication, compassion, loving, and kindness both for myself and the people around me. I was going nuts internally as if someone was peeling layers of myself and my identity. I wrote my mindful friend email after email out of frustration, pain, and maybe loneliness. He replied to all of them and analyzed some of my thoughts. I secretly think sometimes that he probably thought I was crazy, although he is supposed to have no judgment since he is on the path of God. *Oh, well. Back then, perhaps I was a little coocoo, but it was necessary and, in a way, normal.* After all, I was shedding most of my beliefs and facing my internal fears. In a way I was on the same path as he to find my purpose and God in life.

I was just finished with my Mindfulness-Based Stress Reduction (MBSR) classes when the pandemic hit the US in March of 2020. Coronavirus was taking a toll on people young and old. As the duration of lockdowns increased in DC, I was faced with the possibility of being completely isolated from the outside world for long periods of time. To cope with the craziness, I did two things. First, I bought as many plants as I could fit in my space as an attempt to bring the outdoors, indoors. Next, with a group of MBSR grads, we started holding virtual daily meditation sessions. For the entire year, almost all I did was grow plants and meditate on loving, kindness, and compassion. Just the other day, I found the following verse in my journal from the early pandemic days:

There is the world
and
There is an "I"
sitting on the edge of it

I must have felt lonely, ashamed, and imperfect even in my own eyes all those days. Finally, when I peeled enough insufficient layers of my beliefs and unlearned a ton about different topics around my identity, I was ready to love myself fully. The first sign of self-love for me materialized as a healthy sleep routine. Every night, I slept at least eight hours. This way, I was starting most of my days energized, and that was how I became a morning person. Having an extra hour in the day helped me have enough time to do the things I enjoyed. I started writing poetry, checked on my friends, and took extra-long baths with a candle lit.

I only realized the major change in my behavior recently. This past summer, I felt empathy for someone else's pain as they screamed at me out of frustration and called me names. Instead of reacting to their words, I just stood there and felt deep sadness for the pain they were holding onto inside. I surprised myself even more when I prayed for them a few nights in a row. I prayed so their pain could go away, and they could live a happier life. Praying for others had never been a thing I used to practice. It seemed like I had a loving heart, and it was finally shining through me.

Looking at how far I have grown since 2019, I might have become a little kinder. But is kindness enough? *Kindness without boundaries and limits perhaps can also cause pain.* How does one build boundaries? I came back to the present moment when my phone buzzed. "May I talk kindly to others" was the first mantra I added to my phone calendar with a daily reminder at 5:30 pm that was displayed on the phone screen the day I left my old life and my ex. I smiled and whispered, "Indeed."

UNCONDITIONAL LOVE

As I stepped out of the shower and reached for my pastel pink towel with flamingos on it, I smiled at my reflection in the bathroom mirror as she smiled back at me. Marching to the bedroom, I went straight to the closet to grab a change of clothes. I saw a salmon-colored J. Crew top with three-quarter sleeves on the hanger waiting to be picked up. The top was a birthday gift from my brother many years ago. Somehow, I teared up. "Off the cuff," as I remembered my little brother telling me that he spent a ton of time at the mall to get the perfect top for me. He was only a teenager, and the shirt was not inexpensive; *how kind of him to save his money, only so he could buy me a good gift on my birthday.* I couldn't stop my tears.

While recalling the memory of that birthday present from my past, I started crying nonstop at the thought that I didn't thank my little brother enough back then. *I was too self-absorbed to fully recognize his efforts or do something nice for him on his birthdays.* It has been a few years since we even spoke to each other in full sentences. *When did we get so separated?* It all felt as if we were galaxies apart, and I wanted him back. At this point, my tears were unstoppable, and my emotions tumultuous. I missed my little brother so much!

As I stood naked in my closet, balling over a memory, other painful ones started to hit me. As a young person, I remembered how I was unruly, a little wild, and a whole lot careless both about the situations and the people. *Is this happening because of my meditation practice? Am I still in cleansing mode?* All I knew was that right then and there I realized how much I loved my brother and how important he was to me. My beloved Zen master, Thich Nhat Hanh, says, "To love without knowing how to love wounds the person we love." I wondered if my brother ever felt my love for him. I am not sure if I ever showed how much I cared about him the way he wanted to be cared for. With the thought in my mind, I grabbed the salmon shirt he gifted me from the rack of pink tops in front of me.

"To know how to love someone, we have to understand them. To understand, we need to listen," Thich Nhat Hanh said. I never was a good listener growing up nor a retrospective person. In Iran, everyone knew their place and behaved accordingly, and so did I. But something about being alone and trying to find my way in a whole new country taught me and perhaps my family the art of retrospection. I sat in front of my dresser and gazed into the mirror. My reflection again resembled my aunt's round face. We shared the same gaze and black hair. My hands slowly grabbed the hairbrush and I started letting it run in my tangled hair. *Pandemic, man. This hair is desperate for a haircut.* As I continued brushing my hair, I locked my gaze with my reflection. For a second, I couldn't recognize myself. My eyes moved from my hair to my face, neck and fixated on the salmon-colored top I was wearing. I whispered, "Thank you for the top, little brother."

Yet one more tear dropped down my cheek. *How can I show him my unconditional love? Do I even know what that means? Does my family know what that means? Do my parents know what unconditional love means?*

Their elders arranged my parents' marriage. While each has their ways of loving and caring, sometimes I wonder if they truly knew how to fully love and care for each other the entire time they have been married. Did they ever think about different ways the other person could absorb and understand their love? The truth is that I am not so sure if they ever thought of their love life in this way. My siblings and I grew up in a mixed bag of wonderful family dance moments, libraries, outdoor playdates, and an often stressful home environment due to my young parents never getting along. Perhaps, as a result, many of our emotions were neglected both as parents and as children within our family.

Although my parents were huggers and kissers, for the most part, our traditional and conservative culture did not always promote hugs, kisses, or even many heart-to-heart and open conversations between parents and their grown-up children. Growing up, I constantly felt this heavy veil of traditional respect related to age and hierarchy that stood between fathers and daughters. I believe the same went for mothers and sons. The parents and children of the same gender also didn't share every detail about their personal lives. We explored our curiosities undercover and secretly in alley ways and virtual chatrooms. All information about a boyfriend or late-night party had a code name assigned today. When I would leave my parents' house past midnight to party or for a late-night drive with a boy, my sister would monitor the house. She would send a text: "Come home, they are awake."

In the environment I grew up in, talking about sex, money, and our emotions was taboo. One day, I brought up the topic of wanting to have a boyfriend at age sixteen during the family dinner, and my modern thinking and educated dad almost flipped the table. I never learned about relationships, virginity, sex, men, and safe ways to say "no" if someone wanted to disrespect me. *Alas!* All I taught myself was to slap, kick, and scream at the man or, worse, bite their hands and kick their balls, and carry a pocketknife with me when I travel alone. Oh, did I share that traveling alone as a young woman was also considered a pretty unusual thing to deal with for both of my parents and their siblings?

Anyhow, back to my little brother. When it comes to history, philosophy, and ideas, he and I seem to be pretty similar. I do not remember him and I getting into serious arguments ever. Maybe the only time he pissed me off was when he was ten years old. It was the year 2008, and I was studying for the Konkoor, Iranian University Entrance Exam. It is the equivalent of the SAT in the US. Most Iranian students prepare for an entire year before taking this super important test. In a way, our whole life depends on the score we get on this one exam. *Crazy, I know.* During that terrible and stressful year, I had curfews for everything, including the computer screen time and internet usage. However, my little brother was enjoying his summer break from school and had his games all refreshed and re-installed on the same family computer we all shared. Thus, we were competitive around the screen time, and he would alert everybody if I was there off-hours. This is how he, being a little mischief, turned my summer into a living nightmare. *Remembering the little man makes me giggle hard.*

When I think back, I find his five foot some inch little body wearing a big white undershirt and funny-looking pajamas cute and endearing. Even his competitive act to score more on the screen time seems hilarious to me. Such a sweet little asshole he was. *He had such a bright light around him that emphasized his mischievous eyes.* Remembering his ten-year-old self, I smiled. That summer was the only time I remember him being a pain in the ass. Now he is six feet three inches, almost two meters, and can carry me with no trouble. Only now his light seems to be dimmer, and his eyes lack the mischief they once held. *What happened to him? Did we not love him enough? The unfortunate answer to the question above perhaps is yes. I was too concerned about my life and problems and forgot about him and many others. As I drowned in my problems, I left everyone else on the bay. Our family also was caught stranded in many ways, financially, socially, culturally, and more, after coming to the US.* I believe he could use a caring sister by his side, especially after immigration.

"If our parents didn't love and understand each other, how are we to know what love looks like?" said Thich Nhat Hanh. The truth is that perhaps no one taught my parents how to love either. I bet the same is true for my grandparents and their parents as well. *Did they even know what love meant? Maybe they thought their way of love was the correct way.* Many generations of men and women who followed the traditions and respected their elders resulted in children who were brought up functional but not so emotional. *It is time to get in touch with our feelings both for my family and me.*

By this time, I was done brushing my hair. I got up and stood by the chair. "We are going to fix this," I said to my reflection. The chain of emotional neglect had to break somewhere, and I would give it the first crack it deserved. I was going to look out for my family and their healing in this lifetime. With a brush still in my hand, I walked to my desk, grabbed my phone, put my brush on my desk, and texted my brother, "I am thinking of you."

The concept of love and caring for others in a way that they could absorb and understand has been a real challenge for me. I was not sure where to start. *Start with yourself,* my intuition whispered. *I have been working on compassion and self-love for a while now.* Instead of feeling empowered, I felt afraid of the unknown. It has been hard for me to build and maintain meaningful relationships in the past years. I did not feel equipped to hold this responsibility. But I did what I always do when I am afraid: pause, take a breath, and walk right into the scary unknown in front of me. I arm myself with courage, my core competency in this lifetime.

There are many times when I wonder how my brother's life would have turned out if he knew he was fully and unconditionally loved as a child. *I hope that he can still see my love because I am trying to give it a better shot.* Recently, the idea of fully embracing others with everything they bring into our interactions has been at the top of my mind for me. To let others shine as their genuine self and to ask for nothing but the truth of who they are seemed simple but never easy—at the same time, opening up and letting others in can have its consequences and require an exceptional level of feeling safe and trusted. The good news is that if we decide to let others in and accept them for who they truly are, they might amaze us by revealing their uniqueness. *What if I start by accepting who I truly am?*

My name is Golara Haghtalab, and I am the only one in my family who did not change last names after arriving to the

US. Others perceive me as private, cold, tall, creative, and perhaps hardworking. I, on the other hand, think of myself as an achiever of dreams. I speak multiple languages and was born and raised in Iran, the land of art, history, good food, and spectacular nature. Mountains and the ocean both help me feel better, and I love tall, dark men with fair skin who like to contemplate ideas from an intellectual perspective. I write poems, paint, and enjoy having my nude photos taken by a professional photographer once a year so that I can examine myself better. Fear is my best friend and being courageous is my superpower. I believe, as humans, we have multiple dimensions: spiritual, physical, and mental. The unity and balance of these three dimensions helps me get closer to my best self. What I am not sure of, however, is whether or not I fully love myself.

A few hundred days of meditation later, and I still was not sure if I loved myself. *What the hell have I been working on all this time?* At this point, I wanted a drink, so I went and grabbed the last bottle of my Italian prosecco from the kitchen aisle. *Ugh, bubbly wine will not work tonight. I might need something more potent like bourbon.* Alcohol never works for me anyways unless I am trying to write something deep and complicated. *Does "What is self-love?" count as a deep topic?* I pondered.

According to the author and psychotherapist David Richo, love is grace. Loving ourselves with our spiritual holes, mental and emotional voids, and trauma altogether means giving ourselves grace. Grace is love. I am loved. Simple but not easy. *If I can love myself in this way and do it again for others, we could all be in a loving relationship. What if others never learn how to love me back? In that case, I have done my part and will continue doing it.* Bingo! I had a solution.

Sipping away on my fancy drink in its fancy glass, I reached for my phone. I had a text message from a potential romantic interest; *wow, how dare he text me this late in the evening? We are in a pandemic anyway; what's the point?* I decided to respond to him tomorrow morning. As my emotions started to numb by the consumption of alcohol, I began to get on Instagram. *Oh boy, I better watch out to not drunk post anything on here.* Luckily, my attention was shifted from the never-ending feeds by a phone call. It was my little brother. He was calling to say "Hello!" While on the phone with him, I took a mental note: "Unconditional love starts here."

PART 3:

ROOTS TO
THE EARTH

—

MARGE

——

Woman
I am
My wings are hidden from the eyes
Though I fly
From time to time
In all horizons of history
Looking like a symbol
Shining like a firefly
Briefly
Although
My presence is longer
Covering the beginning
And the end of humanity
I am
Woman
Sitting here since Eve in bible
Hava in Quran
Bearing children
Guiding wars
Ruling countries

Yet kept unknown
Yet marked unseen
Yet perceived as weak
For that
May gods fuck all of you.

I journaled in the same notebook on my desk. *I am on fire this evening with my writing.* After a quick reflection, it was time for some tea. I was feeling a little sleepy after having dinner and went to brew myself chamomile tea. As I stood in my quiet kitchen, I felt the loneliness creeping into my body and mind. *Happily single.* I tried to remind myself of my contentment as I poured the hot water into my favorite green cup with dogwood flowers painted on it. Announcing my state of happiness regarding my relationship status did not thoroughly shake off my thoughts. Suddenly, a long train of thoughts and memories hit me. I have been single for more than a year. Memories of my last serious relationship marched in front of my eyes. My mind went through all the details from beginning to end in a time that seemed like a blink of an eye. Strangely, the review of my memories did not stop with that relationship. I stood there as if I was hypnotized, starring into the unknown with many memories marching in front of my eyes like soldiers on an important mission.

One by one, the images of men I dated paraded in front of me. My mind dared to travel in time, further into the past and reveal other forgotten details of my history. Finally, everything paused for a moment in time. It was the year 2005. I was sitting on my grandmother's (mama) terrace the morning after witnessing my grandfather's (*bava*) passing in the small room. I was only fifteen years old. When my *bava* passed away, he was surrounded by his eleven children, more than thirty grandchildren, and many of his close friends and relatives. *Such an honor.* From where I was sitting on the terrace, I could hear my uncle's voice asking my grandmother to make decisions about the funeral. She struggled with each decision she had to make.

My mama was only nine years old when her parents promised her to my grandfather, perhaps a teenager, seventy years ago. The age difference between mama and my great uncle, her firstborn, is only fourteen years. I do not know my grandmother as much because her sweet, wise, and calm nature over the years covered up many of her feelings, thoughts, and opinions. I never saw her behaving out of the societal norms surrounding her role as a married woman. In her world, my grandfather was the person who worked outside and made important decisions. Mama, on the other hand, kept the house and nurtured their children. So, it was only natural for her not to know how to make decisions after *Bava*'s death. As she became the head of household, in a matter of a day, my grandmother's pitch-black hair turned gray under the pressures of the world she was shielded from all her life.

Although it seems extreme, Mama's story is not unique or different from the elements of life I've experienced as a young woman both in Iran and even in the US. I have witnessed women in both countries get married and let their men rule the family life for them. On the other hand, I have never been married and am not fully aware of the married life. It seems as if marriage in a traditional sense is not quite for me. Perhaps my understanding of married life is not yet clear to me. Others, however, seem to get married and divorced as easy as drinking water. Divorce also doesn't seem to be my type of thing. Once married, I hope to stay married forever, whether on paper or in my heart.

From time to time, I contemplate a hundred ways I dodged the bullet by letting go of the men I never married. My realization is often followed by a conclusion that *all I had been doing was avoiding the shot in the past ten years I have been dating.* I wonder what was causing me to keep showing up in front of the bullet to begin with. The answer always is that I wanted to live the independent life of a modern woman while following the traditional path of finding a partner. In a way, I wanted to both be my grandmother and Gloria Steinem. Well, the two are incredibly different from one another.

In Iran and within my traditional culture, marriage is sacred and holds a high value in the list of accolades a woman or a man can gain in their lifetime. My people have based couple's unions on tribal and family relations, power, security, and a girl's beauty for many generations. Before arriving in the US, I thought only my folks made logic the core of their decisions for tying the knot because almost all American movies showed us that Americans marry purely for love. Ten years into my American life, I have seen people here consider logic more than anything when picking a long-term partner. Then, they try to fall in love with their logically chosen match. "Trying" seemed to be the keyword here. Men and women try to make the best logical decision for themselves about marriage and then see if they will fall in love. To this day, I have not seen a person marry someone they are not proud to be with both in the US and Iran. Where does that pride come from? Americans seem to put a lot of pride in their careers, the location and size of their houses, and in some scenarios, education. Traditional Iranians, however, seem to value honor, family reputation and wealth, and the bride's appearance above all.

Just the other day, I was chatting with my dear friend Liz about the characteristics of a successful woman. She is a white American woman who is in love with the Parisian lifestyle. At the beginning of the pandemic, Liz moved to Paris for work. She is the inspiration behind my red lipsticks and the mighty source of all feminist podcasts I listen to. *Liz rocks!* A few days ago, when we were talking about men in our lives, I shared some of my initial thoughts around how the details around marriage now seem to be the same as it was two hundred years ago.

It didn't take Liz longer than a couple of weeks to write up a full-on essay about the topic. In her Medium article, she refers to the once-popular Regency-era romantic series on Netflix, *Bridgerton*. At the beginning of the article, she boldly asserts this statement: "My bone to pick is not with the show itself, which I thoroughly enjoyed and binged in forty-eight hours, but rather with how a society set in Regency-Era London could still so accurately reflect many realities of American society today." Her statement sent me back down my memory lane again.

Close to fourteen years ago, I decided that it was time for me to try out my first serious relationship. I was sixteen years old when I first asked my parents if it was okay for me to have a boyfriend. Since dating is taboo in my culture, I expected my dad to lose his temper at the thought of his little girl thinking about having a boyfriend. But I hoped to have his blessing. He never granted it. After observing my parents' reaction to the topic, I decided to go ahead and pick myself a generous, tall, dark, very cool, and smiley boy, nonetheless. *I was curious.* Once I started dating my first boyfriend, my conservative and naïve view on dating resulted in me expecting marriage from him one month into our relationship. *Crazy and sadly hilarious. Like, what the hell was I thinking?* Although I finally decided not to marry the first boy

I dated, my story was not any different from the experience of courting in Regency era depicted in the Netflix series.

Based on what I remember in Iran, the dating itself, and everything else that led up to it and came after it, is no different than the way things were back in 1813 London. The similarities in details even covered mamas trying everything to secure the best match for their daughters within upper-class circles of the society. As I continued reading Liz's article, I caught myself thinking, *Even today, if a woman marries someone who belongs to higher circles of the sociality than hers, it will be counted as a bonus point.* I fascinated myself with this thought, but quickly another thought clouded my mind. *In the past few years of dating, I dodged many bullets.* The reason why perhaps was hidden in the truth that all these years, I have tried to be both my grandmother and a modern woman in all my romantic relationships. Perhaps this is why I constantly got in front of the bullets and managed to dodge them. *How did I go from loneliness in my kitchen to the topic of courting in 1813 London, again?* My thoughts were once more back in my body as I stood in the kitchen. With my hands, I gently grabbed the cup of tea and walked to my pink couch.

Looking back at my life, I admit that dating was no easy task for me because I had to trust people and wear my heart on my sleeve in a culture that saw romance as taboo. Just the action of seeking love, and God forbid a lover, for a woman like me required a great deal of courage, because dating, to me, was portrayed as harmful. My parents were born and raised in a conservative Turkmen Iranian family and, for a long time after our arrival to the US, had their minds set on how a proper young woman must behave in the society. When we first arrived in the US, they knew almost nothing about the ways of the new culture that promoted premarital dating. It did take them closer to ten years before they realized that, maybe, they should reconsider some of their initial beliefs about relationships, marriage, and perhaps the meaning of love.

When comparing my family to many other families with similar backgrounds to ours, I consider my parent's decision to course-correct their thoughts on love almost heroic. They decided to change their old views, and I know that was not easy for them, especially at their age. It took us ten years, but eventually, we all learned that traditional dating methods would not work for a modern-thinking woman or man. Independence and financial stability do not always attract a conventional man to an independent woman. *Surprise!* We had to expand our thinking and our options to find lasting love into alternate and sometimes unknown horizons with fear riding in the backseat all along.

The key to finding love, I finally learned, was to know myself and my values. When I started to realize that I could only be enough for myself, yet a new realization hit me on my forehead. I discovered a great void in my life. *I was thirty years old and knew nothing about myself. Who am I, and what do I like? Does being in this country for ten years make me American?* From time to time, I think as a naturalized citizen of this country, I must feel comfortable behaving and acting American. But deep down, I do not believe it is correct. Going 50:50 on a date or working insane hours at work is not sustainable for me. The comfort always shows up when I explore more and see myself in a greater context than America and American culture. *How about Golara as the citizen of the world?* I took a sip of my tea and looked out of the windows into the night sky.

When thinking about myself as a citizen of the world, suddenly, all the cultures that I have brought with me from Iran, including the Iranian culture, native culture, languages, clothing, and initial religious beliefs, became part of something greater. They all meant something meaningful to me. This way, I was no longer an "other." From this perspective, due to diversity and differences in cultures of the world, I am encouraged to find similarities between myself and others I meet in preliminary and straightforward details. We are all human beings. Many of us in the world still value the growth of our communities over ourselves. A person from Ghana loves and respects his grandparents and elders the same way someone from India or Japan does. I share having thousands of years old traditions with many African, European, and Asian people. I finally belong.

When I look at my life from this newfound perspective, suddenly, dating and finding a match became much more achievable. I also realized that in a world as vast as ours with many people, finding a husband might be the least of concerns for an independent woman. *Do I want to be married at all? Yes, I do, and marriage will come with its compromises. Will I be happy if I never get the opportunity to be married? Yes, I will be, and my happiness will come with no compromises.* The book of marriage is closed. I took another sip of my tea, closed my eyes, and imagined myself surrounded by peace, happiness, and love regardless of my relationship status. *I shall love and honor myself even beyond death,* I decided.

DEATH

——

imagine million fireflies
light up in the breath of a moment
at the same clearing
you call home

must be heaven
to witness them kindle
send them my regard
such strange flies

so when their light is gone
Like a blown candle
If it gets all dark
Will you call it hell?

In a world
when a word
Sends million fireflies
rushing to your soul

Should we care
To at all dare
In a spur of the moment
Wanting a fairy tale?

This poem-like verse came to me as I contemplated my feelings on endings. *I know the death is truth, and I have questions: Do I know what matters the most for my human life? Is death really the renewal?* It hit me that although I was born and raised in Iran, perhaps my last memories of this life might be developed in this country.

The isolation that came with the global pandemic accelerated my genuine interest in becoming a low-key hermit. Since the pandemic forced us to stay at home, the image of the future has been pretty uncertain. Everything seems hazy, and my mind cannot portray the effects. I also think of the past a lot, especially my hometown and birth country. I remember and think of my relatives and worry for the health and safety of each one of them all day long. Similar to the future, the concept of the past is also uncertain and depends heavily on the strength of my memories. Sometimes it feels like my memories are all made up and never existed. The uncertainty translates into the thinking that I stand on the edge of the world, lost in a majestic fog of a dreamlike moment. Uncertain and frozen, I stand at the edge of horror like a young deer caught in the headlights.

The present moment seems to be the only moment I have. These days, most of my thoughts are around now, the world with face masks, city shutdowns, and restaurants only hosting people outside in tiny plastic igloos. News channels are sharing the death numbers caused by the COVID-19 virus worldwide. The death tolls are nothing less than a scene straight out of a war movie. *Perhaps we are at war with nature.* My thoughts constantly race around the words of disorder, divergence, solitude, loss, resistance, well-being, and healing. I think about the vast spectrum of a person's life from birth to death and think to myself, *This lifetime certainly lasts no longer than a blink of an eye.*

My DC condo is located next to two cemeteries. One of them is dedicated to faithful Christians, and the other one belongs to the national army and celebrates the lives of many soldiers who lost their lives in various wars. Having two graveyards nearby was one of the reasons I purchased my condo. I wanted to remember how natural death and dying are in my life. I wanted to remember death to live and love freely.

There are two cemeteries
By the four walls
I call home
Announcing seemingly morbid news
No one here
dares to hear
Representing brevity
Nothingness
No one-ness
And ghosts
And hidden curtains
And the possibility of other worlds
Or dullness of no worlds
Knowing all of that
I wonder to myself
On all the ways
Yet I still dare to note

My earthly desires
longings
Wants
Not only for myself
But also
for my non existing children too
Agreeing to forget
the nearness of end

I first learned about death and its importance for living a happy life from Cecilia Vicuña. It was the year 2018. I met Cecilia when traveling in New York State. My plan for the day was to stop at the Brooklyn Museum to see the "David Bowie is" exhibit. I first learned about Bowie from my old friend and Bowie Blender radio host, Kelly, in 2012. Kelly was one of my very first friends in the US. She would put on a generous amount of makeup and wore all black clothing. Perhaps she was a little punk back then and I really liked that about her. I took a deep breath and realized that I was in Brooklyn, NY, showered with the creativity David Bowie gifted to the world. I took the show as a sign that I am walking the right path at this point in my life and wandered in the museum.

As I was getting lunch at the museum café, a group of college students and their professor sat next to my table. Soon enough, we started chatting. They were from the Chicago Institute of Art and were in Brooklyn to meet the Chilean artist, Cecilia Vincuña, who had work on show at the museum. "Would you like to shadow the class?" the art professor with a thin handlebar mustache asked. "Of course!" I replied. In fact, I was dying to pretend to be part of the class.

I followed this world-class professor and his students from gallery to gallery where they viewed a lot of art by Cecilia and other feminist artists. Eventually, it was time to meet Cecilia Vicuña in person. Cecilia was a petite, seventy-year-old, yet strong and beautiful, Chilean woman with long gray hair. She was wearing a reddish-brown gown. Her infectious, big smile, however, was the most memorable thing about her. Of course, she came in and sat right next to me on the floor as she told us all about her work, piece by piece until it was time for us to see her installation. As we were walking down the stairs to the gigantic installation, I asked Cecilia, "What is one thing that keeps you happy?" Her response stunned me. She replied to my question by saying, "To live a happy life, remember death. You will be freed." I was frightened and confused but continued walking.

Sometimes, when life gets overwhelming, I take a walk in the graveyards. One day when I first walked into the Christian cemetery, I was intrigued by its grand entrance and fancy family mausoleums. *Wow, even dying in this country is expensive.* Individuals were lying on the ground in an order similar to parked cars at a parking lot. *Grave business seems like a hot commodity.* The strangest part of my visit was that individuals, even after their death, wanted to show their journey by installing unique tombstones. My surprise emerged from my religious upbringing. Sunni Muslims believe in avoiding glorification and adoring graves. I always thought that my people prefer to let the dead be dead as natural as possible.

I believe death or transition does not have to be limited to our actual passing as an alive creator. It can also indicate an end to an event or lifestyle familiar to us while we are still alive. For example, when our plane from Iran landed in Dulles International Airport, my old life ended. A version of me, on the other hand, was born. It took me at least five years before I felt comfortable with my transition and adopted my new identity as an American. I wondered if my family felt the same way about death. My guess was that perhaps not because I am the odd ball in the family.

The other day I visited my family at their new house by the river. My sister and I decided to go on an afternoon walk by the beach. While we were walking and enjoying a lovely sisterly conversation, we saw a dead squirrel lying on the sidewalk. The perished squirrel looked like it was sleeping by the tree in our neighbor's yard in absolute peace. Its breathless body emitted warmth and pleasant energy similar to the one of sunshine. Both its little hands were touching each other as if it was praying quietly with closed eyes. As we walked a little further, I asked my sister if she wanted to go back and examine the dead squirrel. The thought of getting close to a corpse freaked her out in a way that she decided to throw a few conversational punches as a protest.

She tried hard to avoid the conversation or revisit the dead squirrel. Without looking back at what just happened, we decided to continue our walk. Interestingly, the dead squirrels were not giving up on us just yet. As we walked only a couple of blocks down the neighborhood, we saw another lifeless squirrel lying on the sidewalk. This time, the animal's body was completely deformed. Nothing was left of it except some skin and squirrel fluff. My sister avoided the scene again and started showing signs of stress and anxiety. At this point, I could feel her anxiety ghost emerging from its invisible hiding spot. The ghost of anxiety was consuming my sister, so I tried relating what we just saw to the natural circle of life, hoping the conversation would help normalize the incidents in her mind.

"Do you remember the yellow and brown leaves on mom's plants?" I asked.

"Yeah," she replied.

"The brown leaves are usually dead, just like the squirrels we just saw. What makes the animal different from a leaf?" I asked her again.

"Hmmm, an animal stinks and is made out of flesh as we are. Their resemblance to us scares me," she replied.

"Are you afraid of a tiny dead animal?" I asked again. She paused and held my hand between her sweaty palms, tightly. I decided to validate her feelings by reminding her how having fears is natural. "Feeling afraid happens to me too," I said to her. "It is how we react to our fears that can help us move forward in our lives, not the fear itself." I aimed to comfort while encouraging her to dig deeper in her feelings.

At this time of the day, in the afternoon, the sunshine was gently rubbing elbows with our skin, trees, and their leaves. The rays of the sun were providing us with serene scenery that helped calm our nerves. My sister finally opened up about her fears. "I am afraid of instability and lack of safety when a change or transition has to happen. I like it when things stay the same." To gently push her, I started by asking about the way she feels when she experiences fear.

"Would you like to talk about facing the fear you just had of the two squirrels' death?" I asked.

"Maybe we can talk about it on our way back to the house," she replied with hesitation.

Once we got to the lake's small boardwalk, we decided to meditate silently. The combination of sunlight and the lake was adding more magic to the already beautiful afternoon. We sat there for thirty minutes. On our way back home, we stopped by the second dead squirrel. I encouraged my sister to get closer to it. "Remember there is not much difference between a dead leaf, a dead bird, and this guy on the edge of the road," I said to her calmly. She was both afraid and fearless at the same time. My sister gently held my hand in her sweaty palms at first and then held it tighter to the point that I felt a little pain, but I was proud of her as she made her way toward the corpse to get a complete look. I smiled.

I wanted to touch the squirrel to show her how much of its body was already gone, but my sister screamed, "Don't touch it! Don't touch it!" She did not want me to touch the corpse but somehow decided to let go of my hands. I slowly made my way towards the animal's body to allow my sister a little time to sit with her fear. My method worked. She started to surrender. I noticed that her fear slowly diminished. Her voice became calmer. Eventually, it was all silence and curiosity. Examining the first lifeless squirrel did the job. Death was starting to become normalized for her. We started walking back home. I knew in my mind that there was yet another one waiting for us, peacefully with its hands together in a praying motion.

As we came closer to the second squirrel, my sister again started screaming and raising her voice, telling me how much she was afraid of looking at a dead squirrel. Once I reminded her that this was also a normal thing that happens as part of life and to everyone from plants to animals and humans, she again gained control of her reaction. It took me a while to find this one because it was almost blending with nature. Finally, I found it and asked my sister to come to look. She was standing nearly six feet away from me with her face turned to the other side of the road. She was trying hard to avoid the situation. Eventually, she did give in and looked at the dead squirrel lying in the grass and dead leaves. I asked, "Do you see anything?"

She replied with, "A calm squirrel is laying on the floor."

I nodded and held her hands. "Now, concentrate and tell me what else you notice in here," I guided her. Both of us agreed on the strange smell. Perhaps the smell of a freshly dead animal body. "Smell of change is not always pleasant," I blurted out. We both kept silent.

"Once I take my living outfit off, I want to be like the peaceful squirrel," I declared.

My sister kept calm as she examined the corpse with her large brown eyes. After a few more minutes, we decided to move on together and get back to our walk home. On the way back, I asked her if she is scared. She replied, "Because of this experience, I am less afraid of death or anything." Her answer put a smile on my face and added some warmth to my heart. *When we face our fears, they lose the power they have over us*—for my sister and me, facing our fears meant being curious, investigating them gently with hopes to make sense of the unknown in front of us. Whatever the size of a change, fear, and the unknown, it is essential for us to keep our calm and courage to walk through it. All the new and unknown situations does to us is fog up our vision for a moment, and that is all.

WAVES

Walter* said it and I believe
Every piece of art
Aspires to become a song
A static element on the go
Separated from its form
From time to time
Materializing into a spin
On a dancing body or
A mesmerizing sound of a pencil
As it writes on paper
Tales of an unknown flare
In my own dreams even
I wish to become a song
Born out of a wave
Remaining alive
On an edge
Somewhere
In the middle of nowhere

It was about thirty minutes or so that I lived in my own miserable thoughts about the many ways I could have prevented the painful interaction I needed to have with a colleague, tomorrow, from happening. Unable to release myself from the uncomfortable rumination, I scrolled up and down my social media feed, mindlessly, numbing my mind with photos of tropical destinations and cute kittens. Finally, a convincing feeling in my gut pushed me to take a look at my own social media profile for once. On my profile bio, I had written, "Use your power to empower others."

My upbringing within a family in which almost everyone was a teacher, resulted in me being naturally drawn to empowering others. As an adult, I like to believe that a few short conversations with a person is enough for me to see their superpowers and talents. Once I recognize the unique flame burning in others, it is almost impossible for me to stop myself from helping them grow that fire and do something with it. I am more successful in this endeavor at work than in my personal life. For some reason, people are more prone to growth professionally than changing their personal lives. I guess it is easier to not face oneself sometime. No matter whether professional or personal, I believe there is always a way for inspiring others and that is what I want to do with my life.

It was October 2018 when I gave my first inspirational speech. Many people cried and a few more perhaps were touched. I decided to click on the link in my Instagram profile. The link took me to my first CreativeMorning talk. "Thank you for being here," the person who looked just like me said in the video. "Today I am going to talk about honesty. Honestly, honesty is the name of a flower that grows almost everywhere during the warmer seasons. Some also call it the Chinese money plant. I am here, because, lately, balancing the very meaning of honesty by being honest to myself both personally and professionally has been at the top of my mind for me. I also thought you could benefit from learning what I have found on this topic so far," I said in the video.

About eight months before my talk about honesty, I was juggling my day job as an associate chemist at an instrumentation startup with an artist residency at a local festival. My days contained about nine to ten hours at the lab analyzing molecules with microwaves and late-night studio time to build up my installation pieces for the opening night. The upcoming exhibition was called "Who is your RGB self?" The project explored how we use vision to perceive ourselves through the fundamental colors of red, green, and blue. I was excited for this exhibition because it featured a miniature landscape by use of paintings, poems, sculptures, science, and interactive installations to create a fresh perspective on visual self-recognition. I wanted my show to break down boundaries, layers, and defenses we have as people, and flatten our self-images. I thought we had the opportunity to see everyone as three primary colors. This way, we could magnify our unity as human beings. The exhibit, "Who is your RGB self?" had one mission: to help individuals take a short tour into the realms within themselves on a journey from the inside out. I wanted to plan backward while thinking forward to bring my audience's attention to their core: humanity. The exhibit ran for the month of April in 2018.

I am not sure if people did receive the exhibition the same way I hoped for them to understand it. "Artists in San Francisco are doing this work much better," said a passer who stopped by at the opening night. Someone else, however, came into the gallery and screamed with excitement "This is majestic! I love it!" All I know is that some people never understood my work and a few stopped by in awe, admiring its beauty. I knew that art was risky work and its beauty was always in the eyes of the beholder. I was brave to put myself out there and had to be braver not to get hurt by people's reactions. Thinking about what I wanted to get out of the work, I remembered hoping my work could encourage others to ponder something personal to them as it usually does to me. As an artist, I find that each creative endeavor always affects me more than anyone else. So one day when I came out of my space a different person, I was not surprised. One evening, after work, I was just about done installing everything with my team of twin brothers, Collin and Dax, when I unexpectedly questioned myself. *Who am I? What am I doing with my life? Am I happy with the work I am doing these days, or would I want something more from my life?* At that moment, with sweaty palms and a dry throat from the thought that crossed my mind, I knew that I had to be honest with myself.

In the next few days, I found myself thinking about everything I've learned at my job as an analytical chemist. I took on small tasks in chemical instrument sales, marketing, and even in project management. I had a good job and wonderful colleagues and still something was not right. It was about time to let go and find out what I was meant to do. Once the show was up, I decided to leave my job as a chemist and wander the world to find an answer to who I really am. I wanted to learn what I deeply desired to do with the rest of my life.

Two months after my "breakthrough" moment at the studio, I was unemployed. Most of my time was spent in creating and selling art from the comfort of local coffee shops' plush couches. Life would move on as I managed to sell small and some larger pieces of art. One day, however, I decided to stop working on an art commission for a collector. The decision came from a simple source; being a painter was not fulfilling to me. I enjoyed the beautiful colors and each joyful stroke of my paintbrush but painting alone was not enough for me. I wanted something more than being a visual artist. Curious, disappointed, and restless from not feeling whole and true to myself, yet again, I looked for answers or maybe a sign.

Solo road trips do wonders for a restless mind and a searching heart. Less than a month later, I was all packed up and on a semi-solo road trip from Virginia to Quebec, Canada. The experience of driving alone along the east coast was insanely fulfilling. I stopped by the art fairs, museums, and street murals at each corner of Brooklyn, New York, enjoyed a wonderful morning getting brunch and freshly fried, crunchy cannoli in north Boston, Massachusetts, and ordered an original stone baked pizza by the water in Portland, Maine. Life on the road was great and I didn't want to come back to reality.

Along the way on my magical trip, I picked up my sister in Massachusetts and our friend in Maine as we headed to the old city of Quebec. Everything from the world-famous Château Frontenac to the city's rich history, cobblestone streets, and European vibe were a gentle endearment to my heart and soul. Nomadic lives of my ancestors were flowing in me, and I loved being a nomad myself. I soaked in every minute of my time in the soothing city of Quebec and relaxing country roads of East Canada.

Upon my return to Virginia, my heart was wide open, and my soul was ready for action. There was no adventure that I could not take on and no challenge that I would not accept. I was ready for anything! It was time for a new type of art or anything that could make a dent in the world outside of the typical. I could feel my heartbeat quicken with every creative idea and it all became exciting again. When I came across harmonics and the patterns they generate, in a conversation I had with a music professor at UVA, he recommended I investigate Lissajous figures. These figures, also called a Bowditch Curve, are a visual pattern produced by the intersection of two sinusoidal curves the axes of which are at right angles to each other (Al-khazali & Askari, 2012). I had to Google these figures because initially hearing about them simply did not make sense to me. Once I saw a video of these perfectly harmonized loops emerging on the sonic sands, I knew my new creative mission. Lissajous figures were similar to the waves I worked with in the chemistry lab. Art and science were finally united.

The idea of visualizing human feelings into scientific elements in the shape of Lissajous figures seemed fascinating to me. Now that I knew what to use as a creative medium, I wondered about potential execution techniques. This time, it was from my experiences as a chemist that a solution emerged. As a creative soul in a technical field, I did think of ways to translate my artistic feelings into something more tangible. I yearned for a medium that could be understood by scientists and now I had it. Waves are both creative and scientific and they are found abundantly in music and the field of spectrometers. Mirrors, lenses, and lasers were my tools, and I was onto some fascinating shit. It all felt right.

Music is the closest form of art to math and sciences because it is all about resonances and waves. Each wave is a different note. Each resonance a harmony. Because of the connection sound, science, and waves have to physics and music, waves provide a linkage for connecting disciplines of arts, science, and even philosophy. *Art to me is a piece of philosophy.* When I finally realized my creative yearning, I felt like a bomb of energy. For the first time ever, I considered myself lucky to have learned about waves in physics classes at school, during my first job when working with spectrometers, and at the Progressive K-12 Lab where I learned to visualize sound. The word "hello" visualized into what I interpreted as a daisy flower. I was determined to create a stimulus that helped visualize human feelings, emotions, and words into waves.

By following my idea to visualize human feelings into waves and harmonics, more and more I became closer to my authentic and multidimensional self. While from the outside I was working on my passion, inside, I was also feeling wholesome and content. For the entire year of 2018, I allowed myself to be lost in waves, their origin, lifetime, and end where everything becomes silence. Strangely, I started to see myself as a wave too. *Just like a single wave, I too have an origin, and an end. A single dot. If I dare to call my life, the mathematical function with respect to time, when I go through it, my wave shape can become a line, a circle, or even a sphere.* Knowing all of this, I thought that it was time to seriously decide on what shape and form I wanted to live my life.

It is important to note that as humans, we have multiple dimensions: mind, body, and spirit. If I add my feelings and my thoughts into my journey, the figure of my life can become multidimensional and complex. Once my energy levels are elevated, not only myself but others can also feel my frequencies. The physical distance would not matter as much. I learned through my experimentations with waves that the energy of my thoughts can impact others without them even realizing it. So, I wanted to generate the type of waves and vibes that inspired. Just like a wave form, I noticed that my human life also goes through ups and downs and eventually vanishes into air. Waves are generated, almost always, by a source of energy and travel in air based on their energy base until they no longer have power left in them to move forward. Once the source of energy is turned off, there is no wave. This is exactly what happens when we play a sound in a speaker. Once the device is turned off, there is no sound for our ears to hear. The freaky part is that while we cannot hear the sound anymore, its waves might still be around, invisible to our human eyes and ears, floating around us. I started to question how many things exist in the world that are hidden to my eyes. Perhaps a great number.

While the combination and the sum of many things can paint a great figure whether in a wave form or as a painting, if it is not balanced, the entire picture can become a scary mess. To avoid confusion for myself and achieve a balance, again I had to choose how I wanted to cultivate my multi-dimensional self and lifestyle. First, I made a decision to live my life in a way that my thoughts become my protection, golden invisible armor as my friend calls it, and no longer enemies tearing me down. I promised myself to plan on being a complete person in a good way and project outward who I really am. Nothing more and nothing less. *I sometimes wonder if this moment and realization was the beginning of how I became a pantheist.*

As people, we all project outward on who we want the world to see us as. The way we talk, dress, walk, and even introduce ourselves send out frequencies to others around us to portray a certain image. In a way we, the humans, are walking projectors showing off images all the time. I, too, have projected all my life as a friend, student, colleague, and especially when I was being interviewed for a new position. At first, I sometimes thought of myself as an imposter, an empty projection. Later I learned that projections are not always empty. The image we project, at least in my opinion, is what we think we need to be to become accepted by others. We might even have some of the qualities associated with our projections if not all; but how can we know that we are not simply an imposter?

The only way I find out whether or not my outward image was balanced and authentic to who I am, came to me when I finally cultivated self-awareness by meditating. Once I accepted who I was not, I started being okay with who I really was as a person. That was one of the biggest challenges in my life. I learned how important it is to keep track of how much I project outward. Although there are many times I still fail. My favorite question to ask myself is: What is causing me to try and show off something?

I often try to ask myself how much getting these opportunities actually matter to me. Am I allowing myself to come off as someone very different than who I am in order to attract an opportunity that may not fit me? Am I over selling my capabilities? *Perhaps sometimes! As a former people pleaser, I have internalized the skills for becoming who others want to see.* When I make up an image of someone others want to see, I began to get separated from myself. *This is where I start attracting the wrong job, friend, or even romantic partner.* When I lose my authenticity, my projection gains its own life and I might end up living a big mess of confusion, instead of my happy life. When I worked as a chemist at the lab, I was not at all myself. Constantly, something was missing without me even understanding its nature. It was not until I finally came out of my own art show and started questioning my life that I realized the gap between who I was projecting and the real me was an ocean of emptiness and void.

Understanding how myself and others view me was helpful to start cultivating authenticity and integrity. As individuals, we are not always comfortable talking about why we are at a job we do not love, nor are we courageous enough to decide to leave our job if we don't like it wholeheartedly. As a person of passion, I must love my job intensely or be doomed to dissatisfaction and boredom. It's scary to change and get out of our comfort zone to explore the unknown. So, I decided to search for myself in places I had never been: Europe. Less than a month after the road trip to Canada, I flew to Paris, France, for a few weeks of solo backpacking.

With no real purpose other than the intent to learn about myself and perhaps with my mental baggage ready to be let go of, on July 27, 2018, I landed in Paris Charles de Gaulle airport with one black and white backpack filled with only the absolute essentials. In Paris, I stayed in a boutique hotel by the Victor Hugo metro station and in walking distance to Arc de Triomphe. Paris was nostalgic, magical, and home-like. I felt the most poetic in this city because of how much it represented Iran in more ways than I can describe. People, bazaars, and their enormous love for art and beauty could perhaps describe only a few similarities between my home country and France.

After a few days in Paris, I traveled north and met Ger V. in the most orderly country of Netherlands. Ger was a friend of my dear mentor, Grant: a wise, Dutch social scientist with many stories to tell. Him and I met at the PIET HEIN EEK headquarters: a modern furniture shop with offices all around the world including the US. "You are an absolute yellow," Ger commented after I told him about my journey to become honest with myself. "What do you mean?" I asked. "You are an extremely creative person. Art is your freedom and I recommend you dig deeper into yourself by creating and paying attention to the creative process. Once you master yourself, then you can help others," Ger replied. I didn't know what to say next, but his comment gave my trip a new edge, looking deeper into the artistic process.

After spending a few days at a Christian hostel located at the heart of Amsterdam's Red Light District, I flew to Soho, London. I was sick for the entire time in UK's historic capital. London seemed gray and stuffy. When I arrived in Barcelona, Spain, however, my illness faded right at the airport. Gaudi's architecture and Barcelona's weather revived my soul and I felt as if I was a bird flying in the skies of creative energy. Lisbon, my next stop, hit me harder with its Islamic energy and developing country vibes. I remembered Iran again and wondered about my purpose for being there. When I got back to Paris, I paid a second visit to Sacré-Cœur, The Basilica of the Sacred Heart of Paris. This time, I met a French TV personality. We walked down the hill together from the holy place and he basically told me that becoming a star is more achievable than typically imagined. I had no idea what he meant.

I was back in the US at the end of my three weeks. It was on this trip when I missed my country, the US. It was then when I finally learned that I had moved on from Iran, and my home, now, was the US. I missed my country, my home, my new source of energy. When I came back, I knew one thing and that was to touch lives of others with art and co-creating solutions for the challenges of other people. Knowing and acting are two different things, and I was not ready to create anymore. I was tired of the creative scene. What I did, however, was explore solving problems in organizations. This is exactly the reason why I became a consultant, to travel the world and inspire people with my passion. Now that I'm able to be authentic in my work, I finally love my job and most importantly myself.

MENTAL HEALTH

Not all of us need to fit in
After all
The world is
to live in
not to fit in

It is 249 days since March 13, 2020, the day I was told to start working from home. I am starting to see the effects of this quarantine on my mental health as I seem to want to give in to my temper for absolutely no reason at every moment. I also am not sure if this is because of quarantine or the fact that I had virtual school and work all day and every day, including the weekends! The world around me seems low in spirit except for my plants that are out numbering everything else in my apartment—my best investment during this pandemic. I wonder how much green adds to the spirit of my humbly decorated rooms or maybe it is the effect of the Mother Earth Plantasia playlist by Mort Garson that fills the air with an uplifting vibe from time to time. Regardless, I hold all my thirty plants accountable for being the source of joy these days. Life also seems to have better moments when I hold occasional dance breaks in front of my tall and large mirror in the living room.

Along with plants and random dance breaks, it was one of my better decisions to start watching the documentary called *The Universe* tonight instead of all the other cheesy romcom shows that become top hits in the country lately. *The Universe* show reminded me to get out of this earth and expand my thinking onto the greater universe where the pandemic doesn't mean shit! The show helped me ignore the global terror for a moment, though as we moved from one location in the greater universe to another, I realized that right now, I am living in Washington, DC, USA. The world around me swirled and for a second I wondered: *Why DC and not San Francisco? I loved SF far more than any other city in the world.* After a few fog-like moments, I realized that maybe my current state of affairs is the way it is because of the manifestation of the idea I had as a teenager. *Did I manifest my DC life into reality?*

It was the year 2007 when I lived in Iran and there was not a single night that I didn't get to sleep without imagining myself riding a bicycle around the US congress building. It was the year 2010 when a couple of yellow-colored DHL packages bore the news of my mom and I's selection for the US diversity visa lottery. Those two envelopes changed the course of our lives. It was not until November 11, 2011 when we finally arrived in the US and our lives changed permanently.

My first moments in the US were almost magical. Our final destination was the modernly designed Dulles Airport, but the plane had to delay its landing. While we were still flying in the sky as we waited, I looked out of the airplane window down and for the first time saw the colorful and incredible landscape of Virginia beneath the clouds. To this day, I cannot pinpoint the feeling I had when I first arrived here. The first moments in the US sky were surreal especially because it was the first time I was seeing deep orange and red tree leaves from above. Seeing the world from up top made my first plane ride across the globe extremely magical.

To me, traveling across the globe and witnessing magical trees from up above the clouds felt like an event straight from fantasy books. I was not in the world I knew anymore. My eyes were opened up to an alternate world; the parallel universe that modern physicists talk about with its people living parallel lives to mine. *Oh, how different the lives of people are in countries on the other corners of the world in comparison to this one, the land of opportunity.* As the gigantic plane waited, I too impatiently anticipated our arrival on the land that I imagined myself walking on it for many years before going to sleep back in Iran. That day, I decided to believe in wishes being granted. *Bingo! Dream one is achieved! Why not dream bigger now?* I smiled.

My Google Home device was still playing the plant music by Mort Garson and the musical pieces seemed to do all they could to better my mood. Their efforts were working. Cozying up in my coach, I was relaxed and ready for a laid-back night. *It is time for some prosecco.* Although wine is not always a good idea for me when trying to wind down, I decided to stay optimistic. This evening as I sipped my fancy, bubbly, Italian wine, I remembered the conversation I had about my frustrations in America with Vaughan, my mental health counselor. All of the sudden my mood struggled to stay calm. Challenged by the thought of our conversation, I put my wine glass back on the coffee table and sat on my couch. Hugging the pillows tightly for a few minutes, I felt the anxiety ghost rising. Mort Garson's playlist seemed so far and almost muted.

Digging in the past with Vaughan, I remembered feeling irrelevant in the US. My life here and everything I did in my life, the schooling, my first job, becoming an artist, *especially becoming an artist,* seemed to not be enough. As matter of fact, even I was not enough! My social anxiety matched with lack of common knowledge in this new society eventually drove me out of the community I wanted to be a part of. The worst of it all started in 2018, when I started to compare my art with others. What I was doing as a maker, marrying the art and sciences together, did not make sense to myself anymore.

Day by day, everything lacked depth for me. I kept wanting to find something more profound than what I was doing back then, while calling myself an artist. How stupid and random I thought I was by being an artist. I reflected on my travels to Europe as mundane and regarded the effort of searching for something I was unsure of: its reality, my true self, a waste of time. I drove, walked, flew, took buses, rode trains, and hiked, but the depth and contentment were nowhere to be found. Only emptiness greeted me in each of my reflections. I remembered my idle state of mind at the end of my backpacking adventures in Europe. I was in Lisbon, Portugal, looking over the Atlantic Ocean by Sé, a Roman Catholic cathedral that is the oldest church in the city and the seat of the Patriarchate of Lisbon (*Encyclopaedia Britannica*). I was overwhelmingly drunk and dressed in short shorts and plastic sandals, feeling nothing.

Built in 1147, the Sé cathedral has survived many earthquakes and has been modified, renovated and restored several times. *Just like my life and identity.* I found the realization amusing. Remembering the moment in time, I was by the Sé, sitting on the edge of the cliff. Thinking back on my drunk-off-the-Portuguese-red-wine self, I realize that I was not serene at all that day. In fact, I was really going through life with hopes for self-discovery; the hopes that it felt numbed and non-existent. The work I was putting into finding myself was not enough and lacked direction. I was only going from one place to another without pausing or contemplating on what I was learning. So, it was natural to feel frustrated by the process. I wanted to leave and hide somewhere.

After I arrived from my trip and having seen the art of ancient Europe, instead of being empowered, I disappeared from the creative world. The city I landed in was Washington, DC. The marvelous city accepted, greeted, housed, and finally hid me from the world under her transitional layers. I wrapped and hid my painting easel in DC too. I became a very sad nobody, working at a nine to five job that did not suit me. Today, it has been more than a full year since I completed a painting. Grabbing a paint brush still puts the fear of God in me, and the sense that I am not enough to create overwhelms my mind and body. Luckily, my feelings are no longer strange or scary; however, they persist and do not let me paint confidently anymore. I still do not know how to improve my ability to create again. I feel lost in the US, and I need to be found.

I arrived in the US already an adult with a developed sense of self. My identity was shaped based on my life back in my small town filled with people who looked the same as myself and shared the same collectivist culture. Our mutual traditions and background, even our language went back to thousands of years. Imagine being a twenty-year-old girl, living in a bubble with a unique, almost indigenous culture and then have the opportunity of traveling across the globe to live in a first world country. The whole thing was a time travel experience for me. I travelled at least seventy years forward in time when I landed with that airplane that brought us here. My identity was irrelevant in this new world. *I was irrelevant!* The air in my room felt heavy, and I could no longer hear the music. I sat in a self-created silence for a few moments with the ghost of anxiety hovering over me.

My thoughts went to Charlottesville, Virginia, the town I call my hometown these days; the place we first called home back in 2011. Even to this day, the Blue Ridge Mountain reminds me of the ancient mountains of Alborz in Northern Iran and the three-hour trip to the edges of Atlantic is our new road trip to the Caspian Sea. Virginia's orchards are the more structured version of orchards in north of Iran where I grew up with the imagery of farmers picking apples every fall. As a child, my dad and I would go to the orchards and farms on his bike to buy some fresh fruits: apples, oranges, and melons depending on the season. Although Virginia doesn't have watermelon, saffron, or pistachio farms, it is still the closest unknown to what was known to me in the old world. The geographical similarities made it even easier for my already developed young adult self to initially think not much has changed with our immigration other than my language. But I was so very wrong!

I learned more about the world around me when enrolled full-time at the Piedmont Virginia Community College. Throughout my college days, I continued working part time. Holding multiple jobs in many layers of the society helped me learn English, but I failed to learn about the culture. In earlier years, my mind was still unable to make sense of the bigger picture. All I could detect was a sense of otherness. I was naïve towards the true culture of this country and failed on picking up on subtle signs of elitisms, racism, and xenophobia. People at the community college were more like me than not. My obliviousness toward the subtle signs of differences between cultures prevented me from realizing the fact that things had changed since we left Iran, and for that I have to change too.

After graduating from the community college, I was fortunate to study at the University of Virginia, one of the most respected public schools in the world, and I was fucked! My low level of English proficiency in comparison to my peers at UVA summed up with my inability to understand the social norms set me up for a serious failure. First semester in, I was put on probation only because I didn't know that I must stay enrolled in a certain number of credits and not drop below that number. The side jobs had to go as I struggled with my grades gravely and I needed to balance my stress level. Things got even crazier when one of the people I respected the most told me that "studying chemistry at UVA is for bright kids" and that I should study poetry and arts instead! I knew right then and there that whatever it took, I had to graduate with a degree in chemistry from this university to prove myself that I, too, was a bright person.

For days after my interaction with this person, who respectfully called arts the thing of those less bright, I was angry. For the first time in my life, my rage was activated against a stranger. I wanted to yell at him and scream that "he is a lunatic for having such a low opinion of me and the creative world, while not knowing that I got the highest grade in my class back in high school for chemistry!" He didn't even ask what I studied back in Iran. I screamed to the wall in the backyard of my dormitory. "Goddamnit, I took more math classes than your AP students!" I threw a rock. "The only difference I have with others is that my mind is foggy and I do not understand the fast-paced clicker questions." I threw a bigger rock into the darkness, before kicking the wall. "I will fucking show you who is bright, you fool!" was the last thing that came out of my mouth before I threw one more rock into the darkness and vanished from the backyard.

Now that I think back, my anger at this person was one of the first signs of the internal shift of identity that was happening inside me. Four years later, at the graduation ceremony, I saw him greeting transfer students. I walked right to him. "Do you remember once you told me that chemistry is for bright students and art is for less bright? Today, I graduate with a degree in chemistry and another in arts." He replied with, "I am glad you didn't listen to my foolish comment" and opened his arms to give me a hug. I decided to let go of my frustration and we hugged in the middle of the UVA lawn.

There is still
A fiery teenager in me
Fighting her demons
Swimming upstream
Like a salmon
On the path of
Up the stream movement
I feel the emotions of an enraged teenager
Leaking into the reality of an adult woman
As punk as it gets
Presenting not only the young anger
But also
Raw emotions of an ambitious woman

Yet to free herself
From her old demons
At least I am aware
Aware, aware, aware
Of my duality
Not only dark but also hopeful
Knowing that awareness
Is the first step to freedom

I remember feeling accomplished that day at the graduation ceremony. All the pride and self-confidence, however, vanished in 2018 especially when I visited my last stop in Europe: Lisbon, Portugal. To get to Lisbon's Sé Cathedral I had to first get on the cable bus to take me up the mountain. On my way up to the Sé, I stopped to get food and lost my way in the small and weary streets of the ancient city. As I struggled to find my way back to the Cathedral, I found small and hidden ceramics shops in the heart of the mountain accompanied by wonderful cafés by Lisbon's most scenic observation decks like Miradouro das Portas do Sol. In all these locations that I came across by chance and with struggle, I stopped. You can drink on the streets in Europe. So, I saluted my wine to everything adventure brought into my life that day.

It is safe to say that I drank my way to the cathedral. Among many gems on the road, I also stumbled upon the National Pantheon, *yet another church*. The Pantheon was different from others because of its architecture. It was painted white and had a dome, similar to the Islamic mosques in Iran and Turkey. "I bet this whole religion thing is all connected, and they are not telling us," I murmured to myself. Lost, drunk, and without realizing back then, I was living a very honest life with myself at the moment. I was enjoying everything my adventure had to offer like a wave moving on its path.

Just about two months after I was back again in the US, I was giving a talk at a local CreativeMornings chapter. The theme of my talk was about honesty. All I remember from that moment is my mentor's warm presence among the audience and people's emotional reaction to what I had to say about waves. I told my audience that day something along the lines of waves being the most honest, dynamic, propagating forces that disturb the reality to find their own way. And I compared my own existence to a wave with an origin. People cried.

I couldn't understand the reason behind the tears. All I knew was that I might have touched something in them that felt genuine. *What am I feeling now that I unpacked all these memories?* I realized the simple act of reflecting on the past, helped me learn and grow from my journey to self-discovery two years ago. It seemed as if my self today was helping me better understand the things of the past. *Patience little bird, patience. Everything is going to be alright.* I attempted to calm my vulnerable, yet magnificent, beautiful, and unbelievably human immigrant self, sitting on that pink coach in Washington, DC. It worked!

UNEXPECTED

———

Unleash thee...
There are no others here
It's only you and I

I was cozied up on the coach when my phone's screen lit up. It was a photo of a steamy Italian dish, risotto. "Toto!" I grunted! *Ugh, I told him to stop sending me food photos... his photos remind me of my loneliness for some reason.* The image of the freshly prepared risotto looked yummy. I could almost imagine it to be real, so with no hesitation, I "hearted" the iMessage.

Toto is one of my dearest pandemic friends who lives on my last nerve from time to time. Half American, half Italian, this gentleman mostly poses the Italian attitude he grew up with back in Italy. Everything is sensual and perhaps sexual to him, especially when it comes to food. With each food photo he sends me, I wonder, what is the point of sending an image when he can just send me the dish itself. After all, we both live in DC.

While annoying for the most part, Toto still manages to paint a sweet image of himself in my mind. Most of our interactions include bitching about our lives, getting into arguments with each other over anything under the sun, and being forced to meditate during our trio sessions with Max. While we only met a few months before the pandemic, Toto and I became close because of it. His presence helped the deserted life of my pandemic days turn into a beautiful oasis filled with prickly but flowering cacti. His warm but virtual friendly embraces from time to time, delivered in his one-word texts "hug" meant to comfort, have been the highlight of our heavily virtual friendship.

During the pandemic, I made four virtual friends. I never met the two ladies in person ever, Miriam and Eilis. Max, Toto, and I met only a few months before the pandemic lockdowns started. It has been impressive to create and maintain these relationships virtually. *We adapt.* As for my introvert self, however, I have been loving it. Miriam and I met at the book-writing class, and I fell in love with her book about women's menstruation. Eilis and I met over an entrepreneurial event where we both were part of a focus group. I met Max during the Mindfulness class we took together pre-Covid. Toto attended the same event I ended up at completely by chance.

I still remember the day I met my Italian friend. It was a cold and icy day in November of 2019. I was just separated from my partner and was feeling all the gloomy feelings associated with a major heartbreak. Earlier that day I finally decided to call a cab and make it to the Center for Mindful Living so I could attend a meditation session. No matter how I felt, I decided to get into the car and go from point A to point B, thinking that would be easy. Once I got into the cab, my driver started the conversation. Just like any other friendly person who enjoys a good chat, he attempted to ask about everything in my life. Surprisingly, I found myself answering his questions and letting all my feelings out. Perhaps, I felt comforted in knowing that he did not know me. At the end of our trip to the center, he turned to me and said, "Time heals everything." I got out of his cab with a "thank you" and a half-assed smile.

As I walked toward the center, I could see a paper glued to the door with a big word "cancelled" written on it. I just wished that it was not the session I came for that got cancelled. Right in the midst of my wishful thinking, one of the staff members came out of the center and informed me that the 3:00 pm session was now cancelled. I could feel rage bubbling inside my chest and immediately spreading into my throat, head, and stomach. Without paying attention to his comment, I went inside. Part of me hoped that he was wrong.

"The website does not reflect the cancelation. I have traveled across the city to get here for nothing." I said to the staff member while visibly in pain and disappointed. Thankfully, in a mindfulness center, all emotions are welcomed, and I was not judged by anyone in the room. Sherry and Dean, two of the volunteers at the center, were kind and attentive to my frustration. Dean sat next to me and listened for understanding and Sherry suggested I make myself a tea. With a cup of herbal tea in one hand and a calmer nature, I sat in the Lotus room waiting for the next class as per Dean and Sherry's recommendation. From the class description I had no clue what to expect. All I knew was that I didn't want to leave the center, as its calming environment I found soothing.

Maya, the evening shift volunteer, knocked on the door of the Lotus room and with a calm voice greeted me, "You must be Golara. This class is going to be fun. The team is great." I followed her into the larger meditation hall at the end of the hallway. The room was empty and lit with the afternoon light coming in from the windows at the end of the hall. After getting settled in the space, I sat on our yoga mats in the large room and waited for the chanting team to arrive. Maya and I were deep into conversation as I told her about my life in detail, when a tall young man with a beard and a candy stripped pattern turban, large speakers, and music instruments entered the hall.

For a second, the man's appearance and tools left me speechless as I couldn't make sense of what was happening. The whole situation became more confusing when a woman with a giant guitar showed up in the room as well. I wondered if I accidentally signed up for a concert. If so, that would be way different from the session I came for, a contemplative view of the current political system in the US. After all, the former pedagogical session had nothing to do with cacao, music, and a group of hippies. Perhaps, however, this musical session was what my soul really needed that day. The class started at 3:30 pm sharp. We were going to chant, drink cacao, and do yoga, simple as that.

Before, I knew it, there was about twenty of us sitting cheek to cheek in the meditation hall, chugging our cacao drinks and chanting, "Shiva, shiva, shiva, your love is my medicine!" The woman with the guitar and an angelic voice was guiding the chanting and the man with the turban refilled our mugs every so often with warm ad earthy cacao. The whole thing seemed absolutely bizarre to me. Everything became even more fascinating when I found myself bursting into tears as the chanting and meditating continued. I was touched by the processes and was sobbing on the floor as I was guided to perform a child pose.

What the hell, this is so embarrassing. When we were guided to sit and share a word as our "medicine," a man around the age of forty-five was still laying on the floor. *Maybe he fell asleep?* I was proven wrong when it was his turn and he grunted, "Orange!" as his medicine! *What the hell!* I totally judged him and his medicine of choice because "orange" sounded weird and irrelevant. He never bothered to get up and sit instead he continued to lay on the floor. The dorky guy with orange as his preferred medicine of the day was named Toto.

I cannot fully comprehend how Toto and I stayed in touch, nor remember how we became friends. I am sure, the pandemic and our shared interest in poetry had a full influence on the materialization of our friendship. Initially, exchanging the works of eighteenth-century romantic poets such as John Keats and William Blake defined the depth of our interactions. With extension of lockdowns due to the pandemic, Toto and I bonded over the challenges of staying home alone, the discipline of our daily meditation sessions, random food pictures, and eventually our state of mental health. We only met for three times this year and each time it was to enjoy the nature, one of which was at the National Arboretum.

Toto and I met up on a Saturday after one of my long weeks. It was exhilarating to finally be out of my apartment and in the beautiful gardens of the Arboretum. We parked our cars at the Holly and Magnolia parking lot. Toto and I walked to the Asian and Chinese gardens. We passed the beautiful magnolias, rose bushes, and trees to which their names were mystery to me. I found these sections of the park particularly beautiful because of the iconic and delicate vegetation they preserved.

Even in reality, Asian plants are like ink paintings and in a way very poetic, just like my friend's soul. The walk was awesome and, in a way, majestic as it allowed me to tap into the grand amount of beauty that is hidden in the heart of nature. The Asian architecture in the park also added to the palette of all things serene. At the intersection of the Asian and China Valleys sat a single Chinese pagoda-style gazebo with red columns and a grey-green roof overlooking them both and the winding path to the China Valley. It was paradise on earth.

While enjoying the walk, I saw the visible amusement in Luka's body language as well. He would move around a plant about ten times before capturing a shot that satisfied his need for perfection. He was enjoying the beauty in the details as he captured picture after picture with his camera. From time to time, he would be frustrated and complain about how the camera lens couldn't capture the beauty in front of his eyes exactly the way he wanted it. *He is like me, only the male version, Italian, and balder.* I giggled at my thought.

Although poetry and love of nature are two things I appreciate about Luka, there is one thing about him that is completely out of this world. I believe he can see people for both what and who they are. This is because Luka naturally prefers to observe, ask questions, and listen. His ability to observe others and their behaviors closely even helped me realize something critical about myself.

It was close to the year mark since we first met, when he and I got into a painful argument over boundaries and respecting each other's time. Mainly, he was mad at me for asking too much of his time. "You ask way too much of my time by expecting me to read your writings," he said. "Well, you are the literature person, and I am not confident in my English writing," I replied. "I edit for work and that is a job and comes with a serious price tag," he added to his argument before wrapping it up by saying, "You have no boundaries!" I hung up the phone on him only because he was telling the truth and I didn't want to be there to hear it.

Two days later, he called me up on the phone and started asking me questions about my attachment styles. "I am not your girlfriend, Toto. Take it easy," I replied over the phone. "Do you know what attachment styles are?" he asked. "Nope," I said. "Attachment styles refer to different ways people relate to others. There are four styles: Secure, Anxious-attachment, Dismissive-avoidant, and Fearful-avoidant," Luka explained kindly. I did not know what my style could be that night but sure thing I researched it after we hung up.

Because of his observation and thoughtful comments, I decided to learn about my attachment style. After taking an online test and speaking to my therapist, we concluded that perhaps my style is fearful-avoidant. Having this style means that often I am both anxious for affection while avoiding it at all costs. To my surprise, I found out psychologists Nicolas Favez and Herve Tissot, the researchers behind the 2019 study on attachment styles, believe that this attachment style is seldom talked about and not well-researched because it's much rarer than the others. Some other researchers think, however that people like me have the most psychological and relational risks (Agrawal, 2004). As I learned about myself in this way, at first, I was sad. I did not want to think of myself as ill. However much I tried, the stigma around mental health bothered me. My biases were bothering me and after all I was afraid of accepting anything less than perfect about myself. After a few hours, however, I started to feel better for knowing that finally, I had answers to some of my questions. After all, attachment styles are often changeable.

Once I digested the whole attachment style topic for myself, I sensed a warmth permeating my physical body. A smile warmed my heart and soul. I wondered, how unexpected it was to be enlightened by Toto, a person whom I only knew virtually. The one who usually is on my last nerve and somewhat of an asshole from time to time. I was both amazed and confused in the ways the world operates. I stayed in my seat for a little longer, allowing my body to experience the warmth for minutes longer. I felt grateful for the pandemic that brought mindful living and wonderful people like Toto into my life. The cab driver was right: time healed many things and brought in better people into my life.

With yet another sound of a text message, I snapped out of my thoughts and looked at my phone. It was Toto listing out the ingredients for his risotto and boasting about how tasteful it turned out this time. I was infuriated by his momentary ignorance, feeling even more hungry from the conversation about food, but happy for the joyous moment all at once.

there was no God
we prayed and prayed but
the forces of the world
were made out of the sound
waves of our prayers
we were the Gods sitting on
our prayer rugs asking for
forgiveness that was
already given

PRAYERS

———

I shielded my eyes with my elbow as a blinding light flooded my vision. The light at the end of the alley was only the headlights of a car driving through it in my direction. It was odd to see the light coming towards me; it felt like a holy event for a short moment. It all faded away as I saw the car as it passed by me moments later. It's been a few years since the concepts of light and darkness got clouded and mottled in my mind and heart. Thinking about what is right or wrong is resulting in confusing thoughts that touch the present moment more than I can comprehend. Most times I am not sure of my purpose in working so hard to achieve. What is it that I am trying to prove? Who am I trying to keep happy? For many years I did not know the answer to any of these questions. Even today, I was unsure. The entire walk back home from the gigantic recycling bin across the street, I thought about many questions that flooded my mind.

As I kept track of the wandering thoughts about life, light, and the source of my ambition, I unlocked the door to my condo and walked into my place. The clock on my iPhone's screen showed 10:35 pm. *It is time for bed.* As I laid on my velvet couch in the living room, I looked out of the window. Everything was black and all I could see were the lights of the airplane flying in the sky. I wondered about the travelers inside the plane and wondered whether or not there were any immigrants among them. My body felt tired, my mind was unclear and foggy, my spirit wanted to fly into the sky. I was all over the place with my thoughts about the reasons behind my over achiever personality. Perhaps, one was to impress others.

Suddenly, a thought hit me. *What if I could be careless about everything and anything in the world, including money, prestige, and other people's validation, what would I want to wish and dream for? What would be the things I would pray for having?* Although this was not the first time I asked myself this question, this time it felt even more challenging for me to answer it. Maybe I was too tired. It could also be that I wanted to avoid the question because that would be the easy option. So, I sat there on my couch and thought of my priorities for a moment.

A few minutes later, I got up and looked for pen and paper in the middle of my dark room and under the moonlight creeping into my living room. I finally made it to my desk and turned on the desk lamp, "Aha! Got you, damn pen."

I started my writing with a question: Do I believe in whether or not wishes can be granted? My answer followed: Abso-freaking-lutely! Very soon, I had a long list of pretty silly and sometimes out of touch wishes purely based on my stream of consciousness.

- I wish to have philosophers, human rights activists, and poets who share the same vision as I for dinners at my place.

- I wish to be wealthy enough so that I can donate a great bunch of it to causes that support women and children.
- I wish to die a clean death in my bed with a full belly, perhaps after having a dinner party with my loved ones; after we talked about our past memories and laughed and ate and sang songs and danced.
- I wish to be happy with what I have and stay out of feelings of envy and jealousy.
- I wish to see the world becoming a better place for all of us human beings, plants, and animals alike.
- I wish to see my sister blooming with her talents.
- I wish to see my brother thriving in his life.
- I wish to live a cheerful and joyous life every day.
- I wish to eat Iranian breakfast in the backyard of my house every day of every summer.
- I wish to laugh and love harder.
- I wish never to forget the lessons of 2020, however good, bad, and the seemingly neutral ones because this year was a great year for human beings to learn about themselves.
- I wish to become an expert in something.
- I wish to work part time and still keep my lifestyle.
- I wish to believe in myself and my ability to make the right decision most times and be okay when I don't make the right one all the other times.
- I wish to keep my serenity in three dimensions of mind, body, and spirit.
- I wish to find the best romantic lover someday who understands and cherishes me just the way I am.
- I wish to love the weak, the poor, the disabled and continue to help others grow and become empowered to the best of my ability.
- I wish to care for people's pronouns.

- I wish to make more gay friends.
- I wish to stand up for a Black person and injustice.
- I wish to speak kindly of others with kind words and gentle sentences.
- I wish to have boundaries to protect my peace.
- I wish not to be afraid to do the right thing not only for myself but also for others.
- I wish to write and finish up this book I started.
- I wish for my book to be successful.
- I wish not to chase anything that is not meant for me.
- I wish only to keep relationships that are like rain and natural, where I am comforted, listened to, and seen.

The list went on and it was about an hour later when I had finally written enough. I realized my wish list started with outwardly positioned wishes and became more personal towards the end. I gave the whole list one more read. *What am I looking for?* Perhaps I want to be happy, helpful, and loved. The most interesting wish was the one that I wanted to work less. Up to this point in my life, I thought of myself as a workaholic and this wish was telling me the opposite.

Looking at the long list of "wishes" I thought to myself about the ones I wanted to pray for having. At this moment, I had to define for myself the meanings of prayer and hope. What does it mean to pray and how do we know we are hopeful? Are those two words practically the same? It was about midnight now and I continued writing in my journal; hope is the thing with feathers and prayer is the feathers with an order from the universe to take the hope to where it needs to go for a wish to be granted. I could now fall asleep.

But my sleep was interrupted by a dream. In my dream, I was elevated so high above the earth that I could see both the planet earth and the sun. Perhaps the time was moving faster than reality because I could see the shifting of day and night happening on both sides of Earth's hemispheres. The whole dream became more strange when I realized that perhaps I was also a planet, a moon, or maybe a star that could observe the movement of the earth from outside. One thing for sure was true, I certainly was not sitting in a spaceship. After observing the movement of the earth, I was brought back on earth and into a dark condo. As soon as I entered the space, the entire place light up. It felt as if my presence caused the earth to move around itself, to make it daytime or simply that I was the source of light. I was not sure.

The apartment seemed all white with a modern design, so I decided to explore. As I walked into its different rooms, I was amazed by the beauty, light, and structure that was there for display. I finally walked into the corridor and immediately gasped! There was a woman on the floor with dark hair and a green and creamy colored patterned tunic. She looked just like me but maybe a hand-made doll version of myself. She was laying on the floor, unable to move with handcuffs on her wrists similar to the ones of slaves. I thought to myself: *In light there is darkness, like this lifeless woman, and in darkness, there is light, like the beautiful place I am in now.* And then I woke up.

When I opened my eyes, it was still dark, the clock read 3:30 am and I shivered. Unable to make sense of it all, I reached for my journal next to my bed and wrote:

- I wish to remain as myself and keep all the dimensions I have as a person.
- I wish to remember my heritage, grandparents, and my origin.

- I hope to build a bridge between the new world and the old world to help myself relearn the lessons hidden in each of my experiences.
- I hope to not judge people for any of their actions.
- I hope to live for myself and love the person I am.

I put the pen back on the nightstand and started praying. I prayed for myself, my family, people of DC, everyone in the US, and eventually all people who occupied this earth. I felt content and fell into a deep sleep.

Love
Is a tiny little word
with a big meaning
found in the middle of my chaotic life

I found love
In my heart

Enough for me
Enough for you

Enough for the bird chirping solo
By the corner of this building
I call home

ACKNOWLEDGMENTS

———

During the writing of my book, *Immigrant*, I have received a great deal of emotional and financial support and assistance which I am utterly grateful for.

I would like to start by thanking my incredible support system.

- My mentor, Grant Tate, for his unconditional encouragement and support.
- Miriam Prosnitz for her friendship, comradery, and attention to detail. Her thoughtful encouragement helped me feel, smell, and touch the words I was writing.
- Renzo Reyes for encouraging me to Do It Anyway!
- Hans Manzke for supporting my pre-sale campaign whole heartedly to help my dream come true.
- Morgan Petterson for being the best early-stage reader I could ask for during the revisions and for constantly reminding me why I started writing this book.
- Dan Turello for encouraging me to write poetic stories.

Next, I would like to thank the kind souls I had the pleasure to interview for building a better-informed story.

- Amangol Boghdeh
- Emma Fivek
- Golnar Beikzadeh
- Tenzin Wangjor
- Zeinab Rahnama

I would like to acknowledge the efforts of my editors for being the careful and attentive eyes behind my manuscript.

- Katherine Mazoyer for being my emotional and editorial rock.
- Quinn Karrenbauer for helping me complete a manuscript.

I would like to thank,

- My sister, Parisa Erkin, for illustrations that inspire.
- The book professor, Eric Koester, and his team for allowing me to write a book during the 2020 global pandemic. They provided me with the tools to choose the right direction and successfully complete my manuscript.

I would also like to thank everyone who financially supported my book's materialization into reality. You made my dream come true!

Abby Ng
Abhishek Thakar
Adam Albaness
Ahmed Hassoon

Altun Shukurlu
Amber Lingenfelter
Andrea Bachinski
Andrea Reyes

Annalee Jackson
Anne Herhold
Bavoukidina Apprecia
Brandon Zeman
Bridget Sweeney
Bushra Islam
Caitlin McKelway
Carolina Reyes
Charley Fogel
Chelsea Powell
Chelsea Jeter
Christopher Collier
Claude Elton
Clifton Johnson
Collier Lunn
Connelly Morris
Courtney Mandryk
Dan Turello
David H. Lerman
Divya Ramireddygari
Eilis Wasserman
Elizabeth Nicastro
Emma Fivek
Eric Koester
Erika Chu
Erin Sherman
Faranak Faridzadeh
Golnar Beikzadeh
Grant Tate
Griffin Moore
Heber Delgado-Medrano
Hamid Hosseinianfar

Hans Manzke
Harrison E. Weisberg
Harry Stillerman
Hector Torres
Ian Lever
Ifiok Inyang
Indraneel Samanta
Jalal Erkin
Jen Fox
Jill Parmar
Joe Garofalo
Joe Kacmarsky
John Moody
Jordan & Emily Chambers
Jordan Johnson
Julie MacMillin
Jum Jirapan
Karen Schmidt
Kelly S. Barlow
Khatira Darvesh
Kiara Kishore
Lance Barrera
Laura Jackson
Lauren Hornsby
Lesly Gourdet
Linda J. Wells
Lisa King
Liz Glodek
Magdy Mansour
Mahmood Moghimzadeh
Mana Rasoulzadeh
Maria Ghojoghi

Marissa Mullen
Mary Burns
Mary Quandt
Maryam Razmjou
Matt Minahan
Maximilian Muenke
Mazhar Adli
Melanie Collazo-Espinosa
Melissa Velez
Miriam Prosnitz
Morgan Peterson
Morgan White
Nahid Erkin
Nathaniel L. Galea
Navid Soltani
Nawaz Khan
Neil Sikka
Paige Douglass

Parisa Erkin
Peggy H. Stearns
Philipia Hillmam
Rasheedah Stephens
Reilly Sonstrom
Renzo Reyes
Rina Dukor
Robyn Klem
Rodrick Adkins
Sage Tanguay
Samir Shamsuddin
Sarah Storti
Saul Urrea
Sergiu Mosanu
Sudeepa Thapa
Tenzin Wangjor
Tobe Attah

I would like to thank my parents, Jalal Eddin and Nahid Erkin, for many sacrifices they endured in bringing our family to the US so that we could have what they, themselves, did not have.

APPENDIX

———

Author's Note

International Organization for Migration. *World Migration Report: 2020.* Geneva: International Organization for Migration, 2020. https://www.un.org/sites/un2.un.org/files/wmr_2020.pdf.

Home

Encyclopedia Iranica Online. Vol. XI., s.v. "Gonbad-E Qabus Monument." Accessed May 27,2021. https://iranicaonline.org/articles/gonbad-e-qabus#monument.

Sherwin-White, Susan, and Amelie Kuhrt. *From Samarkhand to Sardis: A New Approach to the Seleucid Empire.* Berkely: University of California Press, 1993.

Swallow birds

Alcock, GG. *Third World Child: Born White, Zulu Bred.* Johannesburg: Tracey McDonald Publishers, 2014.

Languages

Center for Digital Humanities at Princeton. "Ottoman Turkish."
    Accessed May 18,2021. http://newnlp.princeton.edu/language/
    turkish.
Encyclopedia Iranica Online. Vol. XI., s.v. "Arab Conquest of Iran."
    Accessed May 18,2021. https://iranicaonline.org/articles/arab-ii.

What About Fun?

Zaldivar, Enrique J. *Your Unique Cultural Lens: A Guide to Cultural Competence.* Comus: Inspired Pub, 2020.

The Ghost

Geert Hofstede, Gert Van Hofstede, and Michael Minkov. *Cultures and Organizations: Software of the Mind, 3rd Edition.* New York: McGraw-Hill, 2010.

Racial Education

Berger, J. G. *Changing on the Job: Developing Leaders for a Complex World.* Stanford: Stanford University Press, 2012.
Kegan, R., and L. L. Lahey. *How the Way We Talk Can Change the Way We Work: Seven Languages of Transformation.* San Francisco: Jossey-Bass Publishers, 2001.
Patwell, B., and E. W. Seashore. *Triple Impact Coaching: Use-of-Self in the Coaching Process.* Columbia: Bingham House Books, 2006.
Yeganeh, B., and D. Kolb. "Mindfulness and Experiential Learning." *O. D. Practitioner*, 41(2009)

Unconditional Love

Nhất, H. *How to Love*. Berkeley: Parallax Press, 2014.

Richo, David. *The Five Things We Cannot Change and the Happiness We Find by Embracing Them*. Boulder: Shambhala Publications, 2006.

Marriage

Brown, Catherine, and Sarah Shapiro. "Sex Education Standards Across the States." *Center for American Progress*, 19 May 2018. www.americanprogress.org/issues/education-k-12/reports/2018/05/09/450158/sex-education-standards-across-states/.

Fivek, Emma. "Bridgerton is a 200+ Year Old Window into Today's American Society and it's Alarming." *Emma 5K (blog)*. February 11, 2021. https://medium.com/@Emma_5K.

Guest of a Guest. "How To Be Married: Jo Piazza Shares the International Secrets Of Marriage Success." http://guestofaguest.com/new-york/interview/how-to-be-married-jo-piazza-shares-the-international-secrets-of-marriage-success&slide=1.

Waves

Al-khazali, Hisham A. H. and Mohamad R. Askari. "Geometrical and Graphical Representations Analysis of Lissajous Figures in Rotor Dynamic System." *IOSR Journal of Engineering* 2,5 (2012): 971-978. http://iosrjen.org/Papers/vol2_issue5/G025971978.pdf.

Mental Health

Encyclopaedia Britannica Online. s.v. "Lisbon—The 20th Century." Accessed February 26, 2021, https://www.britannica.com/place/Lisbon/The-20th-century.

Unexpected

Favez, Nicolas and Hervé Tissot. "Fearful-Avoidant Attachment: A Specific Impact on Sexuality?" *Journal of Sex & Marital Therapy*, 45,6 (2019): 510-523. https://doi.org/10.1080/00926 23X.2019.1566946.

Hans R. Agrawal et al., "Attachment Studies with Borderline Patients: A Review." *Harvard Review of Psychiatry*, 12, 2 (2004): 94-104. https://doi.org/10.1080/10673220490447218.

CPSIA information can be obtained
at www.ICGtesting.com
Printed in the USA
LVHW041255051221
705332LV00013B/1673